THE EREMITIC LIFE

THE EREMITIC LIFE

Encountering God in Silence and Solitude

Father Cornelius Wencel, Er. Cam.

Ercam Editions
Bloomingdale, Ohio

Nihil Obstat and Imprimatur:
P. Lanfranco Longhi, Er. Cam.
Superior Major

ISBN 978-0-9728132-3-5

Library of Congress Control Number: 2006924016

Printed in the United States of America

CONTENTS

FOREWORD

I wish to express my gratitude to Father Cornelius for the book, *The Eremitic Life: Encountering God in Silence and Solitude*. The author knows the history and theology of the eremitic life, he knows the daily routine of that kind of life, because he chose it for himself. Thus the book is his testimony.

God seeks man, calls him to union with Him on earth and to salvation. At the same time man seeks God, the meaning and goal of life. On the level of appearances, it can be said that the eremitic life means turning one's attention to God and separating oneself from men. Indeed, he who chooses such a vocation places God first but only outwardly separates himself from men. Inwardly he remains close to the Church and the world, close – in Christ – to each person.

A vocation to the eremitic life is a gift for the one called and for the community to which he is joined. But on the other hand, it is a gift for the whole Church. It is a sign that reminds us of God. Every hermitage, every monastery, especially each having a contemplative character, calls to mind: "God is, God is Love. Pause a while, reflect upon yourself, upon your life!" It is like a continuous proclamation of the words of our Lord Jesus: "For what does it profit a man, if he gain the whole world, but suffer the loss of his own soul? Or what will a man give in exchange for his soul?" (Mt 16:26)

1

In today's world, where a person lives in constant haste, chasing after money and subject to manifold pagan influences, he needs moments of calm, reflection, and silence. Contemplative monasteries remind us of that and call us to that.

At this point it is worth citing the words our Holy Father [John Paul II] spoke to cloistered nuns in Warsaw: "It only appears that you are cut off from the world. In reality, you find yourselves right in the middle of it – in the center of temporal reality, in the center of Polish reality – through the mystery of the Church. Behind the enclosure, one does not turn away from people. Behind the enclosure, one loves." (8 June 1987)

I bless everyone who picks up this book. I pray that, under the influence of reading it, many people will find the time and place for a desert experience in their lives. Then they will not only discover God anew but will also discover the road to another person, to a husband, to a wife, to one other, to the community.

—Bishop John Szkodoń
Cracow

INTRODUCTION

A lot of people seem to be looking ever more eagerly for a space of solitude, silence, and prayer. If this is really the progressively anxious desire for meeting the desert environment, and its mysterious awe and beauty, we should not hesitate to take it as an important sign. What it indicates is an uneasiness of the human heart. To a certain extent the uneasiness, as well as the fear and frustration connected with it, comes from the human spirit losing contact with all that is real and true in the world. A sound and wise attitude towards the real is often substituted by the tinsel of glossy illusions. Their insidious charm seduces us away from a clear and sober way of looking at and understanding the world.

It is obvious that today humanity struggles with many different problems and conflicts that are surely going to grow and become even more difficult and that, at the same time, are waiting to be solved. One of the most urgent needs of the modern world is to undertake and face the existential drama of the present time. The call to face it becomes even more acute and piercing because of the great dynamics of civilization and the development of science. We can try to run away and hide from the difficulties we encounter. We can also try to lie and cover up the naked and unpleasant truth about the critical condition of the world. Nevertheless all those attitudes must finally disappoint us when they

3

reveal their childish pointlessness, and consequently their emptiness.

The critical spirit of rationalism, despite all the complexity of faults that it is blamed for, undoubtedly induced the process of liberating humanity from a number of superstitious burdens. However, we ought to remember that the spirit of scientific criticism exposed its own weakness by sowing the seed of new illusions: the belief in the unlimited power of the human mind, science, and progress. Nowadays in post-critical times, human beings have found themselves in a very difficult situation. It is true that humanity has been freed from many illusions that it has been fed on for centuries. At the same time though, paradoxically, people have been immersed in several new, even more dangerous conditions, which make a face-to-face encounter with the world and with others impossible.

So, is it possible to be brave enough to undertake the challenges of the present day? Must serious engagement in the problems of the present day necessarily bring about, as if by definition, feelings of disillusionment, perplexity, and frustration? Before man can get at the essence of his own problems, causing all the different conflicts in the modern world, he needs to put reality into proper perspective to show it in its simplicity and truth. It is impossible to make room for such a perspective without adopting a certain attitude. It is the attitude of relinquishment and renouncement that puts us at a healthy distance from everything we thought we had so far known and loved.

It is very possible that one of the basic reasons why the life of the desert attracts so much interest nowadays is that it is an instrument for equipping the people of today with that wise distance from themselves, as well as from the world of material things. Despite the fact that the desert, barren as it is, is a place haunted by the demon of despair and causes fear and horror, it has always been a shelter for all who sincerely search for the truth. Life in the desert highlights the fundamental tensions of everyday human existence and makes it possible to have an insight into the very heart of a tragedy of the modern world, the tragedy called despair.

The eremitic experience cultivated in different communities, traditions, and cultures has had a plenitude of motivations and forms. For those who entered this way of life, it appeared as a riddle to be solved anew again and again. In the course of centuries the hermit way has brought about astonishment and admiration and, on the other hand, has been laughed at, ridiculed, or has caused irritation. Anyway, it has left nobody cold.

The stir it has aroused has resulted from the wide gap between the choices, aims, and motives of the hermits and the established patterns of life and hampering conventions that have characterized the culture and civilization of their times. The paths of their calling often led them towards new challenges and tasks, which they undertook and successfully achieved. By doing so they blazed trails of personal growth, encouraged new styles in fighting for the victory of truth in the world, and initiated alternative forms of community life. However, the first step of the "revolution" they offered was always taken at the level of their own hearts, and that was probably why it brought such amazing fruits.

Human history throughout the ages is highlighted with the beacons of the eremitic life that shine more or less visibly in different civilizations, cultures, and epochs. Our times do not stand apart in this matter; on the contrary, today we can also meet people who choose solitude, prayer, silence, seclusion, and fasting as their specific way of life. Because they are simple and natural, sincere and open, the modern world seeks them with great eagerness and hope. The Christian tradition almost from its very beginning has cultivated this specific calling that advocates seclusion and love for God as the way of activating and fulfilling the life of faith. The desert is a soil that has been producing the wonderful crop of religious orders and communities, centers of intellectual life and – finally – the most precious fruit of searching for the truth about God and oneself – sanctity.

Initially, the desert was a place of refuge, a sanctuary that protected man from the corruption of the world. For a hermit, the total uselessness, barrenness, and horror of the desert were its chief values. The desert, strange, inaccessible, and even hostile as it may be, frightened away "patrons of fairs and markets" and at the same time it served as a shelter for all those who bent their steps toward finding God and, consequently, finding themselves. The demanding severity of this soil became a hiding place for the brave who had the courage to accept the truth of how fragile and great, poor and powerful, human existence is.

Today, the bare land of steppes and deserts has been conquered; the original place of solitude and silence is now covered with pipes, wires, and roads. At present the desert gives space for seeking money, power, domination, and prestige, not God. That is why the hermits of today are looking for an inner desert of their hearts more than for a concrete geographical location. What they are looking for is rather silence, prayer, and contemplation: the art of communing with the mystery shining in the soul of each person.

I

FROM THE HISTORY OF
THE EREMITIC LIFE

The eremitic movement (Greek *eremia* meaning "desert") has existed in the Church from her very beginning.[1] In the Church there have always been people who wish to devote their lives to solitude, silence, and poverty. They want to do so in order to arrive at the desired union with God and salvation in this radical but simple way. Christian eremitism stems from an elementary inner need of a solitary life, which for some people appears to be the surest way to realize the blessings of the Gospel. A hermit never left the world in order to fulfill his personal dreams of adventure, fame, or individuality. The source of the eremitic experience should be sought, at least in the Christian understanding, in the gift of a calling to intimate communion with God through contemplative prayer.

The anchorites of the early centuries traveled to the sacred places connected with the Old Testament history of salvation. That was also the context of a specific *exodus*

---

[1] Cf. M. Daniluk, "Eremityzm", in *Encyklopedia Katolicka* , vol.4, pp.1069-1078; C. Lialine, P. Doyère, "Eremitism", in *Dictionnaire de spiritualité*, ed. M. Viller (Paris, 1937), pp. 936-983.

of so many men and women who, at the turn of the 4th century, settled in the vast deserts of Egypt and Asia. Often places of their settlement were directly, or at least by an accepted tradition, connected with concrete events of biblical history.

The Fathers of the Church took very diverse approaches to the eremitic movement that so dynamically expanded in their times. According to widespread opinion, a Christian went to the desert in order to follow in the steps of his Master by fasting and prayer, as well as by struggling with the demonic powers of darkness. Origen considered the experience of the eremitic life as an excellent preparation for entering the realm of the Word of God, because it was an opportunity to meditate on and learn the living texts of Holy Scripture. It seems that drawing a parallel between the image of the desert and the inner life of a person who is detached from the world and sin and loves God and his brothers may be ascribed to St. Augustine. For him this difficult path gives, thanks to the grace of mystical contemplation, the chance of reaching a foretaste of heaven. Even in those times when many were undertaking radical forms of self-denial and mortification, the eremitic experience was destined only for the few. In fact, only people of outstandingly strong personality who had already spent a long time on perfecting their ascetic life in a community might dare to choose that path.

What St. Jerome, St. Augustine, and St. Benedict of Nursia put in first place was life in a community. For them the eremitic way was an extraordinary means only possible for those who had long practiced the life of a monk in a monastic community. Theirs was the same approach as the synods in the Eastern Church (Trullan, 692) and in the Western

Church (Vannes, 463; Toledo, 633). Setting communal life as the priority, the synods were often distrustful of eremitism.

1. The Eremitic Movement in the East

The eremitic life took on its specific forms in direct connection with "making a pilgrimage to a desert", a movement initiated in the 3rd century. That process was also linked to the model life of the fathers of the desert, whose charisma radiated widely. The famous sanctity of such great hermits as St. Paul of Thebes (died 341) or St. Antony the Hermit (died 356) attracted many followers. Consequently the first eremitic communities were formed. At the turn of the 4th century they were spreading to the territories on the verge of the Upper and Lower Egyptian deserts. Their hermitages were made from deserted caves or burial rooms, or were built separately. The hermits lived close to each other in small colonies of several persons, but they did not lead a community life. They often settled near towns and spontaneously undertook apostolic work and spiritual counseling for those in need. At the same time, besides the individual forms of eremitic life, bigger hermit colonies were being established. The so-called *lavras* were centered on their charismatic founders. They were founded chiefly in Egypt, Palestine, Syria, Cappadocia (Turkey), Ethiopia, and Greece.

The hermits came from all the social classes. They withdrew to deserted places in order to devote themselves to prayer and mortification. Their ascetic life, which often took on an extreme form, was to protect them against worldly temptations and to strengthen them for their everyday struggle with the powers of evil. They lived by gathering and weaving, but also often accepted alms. The ideal of eremitism according to the Eastern tradition stressed the importance of life in the constant presence of God. The condition called *dispassion* (Greek: *apatheia*), an inner peace resulting from purity of heart, was the sign of such spiritual maturity. It was a basic condition leading to the experience of mystical contemplation.

Byzantium of the Middle Ages witnessed the retreat of eremitism caused by the iconoclastic movement. It forced the hermits to migrate to Athos in the 11th century. There, along with the tendency to build communities, a form of the eremitic life practiced jointly in so-called *sketes* developed. Some lived also as individual anchorites in independent hermitages (called *kalivi*) or in rock caves. The sacred mountain of Athos was the place where the idea of hesychasm was adopted anew. It was related to experiencing inner solitude up to the point of reaching complete silence and peace. The idea is based on practicing the prayer of the heart, a kind of inner prayer leading, by means of synchronizing it with one's breathing, to a constant unity with God.

In the course of time the tendency to live in seclusion became connected with several sophisticated forms of mortification such as living in a barrel, wearing chains, or staying on exposed platforms (those hermits were called stylites). As the eremitic life developed, a way of separation called "reclusion" appeared. Its followers, as prisoners of Christ (Philem 1:1-2), were shutting or even bricking themselves up in their cells.

A specific type of Eastern ascetics who also practiced the eremitic life were the so-called "elders" (Russian: *старцы, startsy*) traversing Russia in the 15th and 16th centuries.

At the end of the 18th century the followers of Paisius the Great reestablished *starchestvo* (Russian: *старчество*) in Sarov (with the famous Seraphim, who died in 1833) and in Optima Kozielska (with Ambrose, who died in 1892).

2. The Eremitic Movement in the West

The 4th century was the time of the blossoming of the eremitic life in the Western Church. That was when the great Athanasius wrote his biography of Antony the Hermit and when hermits appeared in Italy and the neighboring islands. Around the year 360 Martin of Tours founded an eremitic village for 80 people, priests and laity, at Marmoutier. At the same time many hermitages were being established in Gaul. They may be characterized as combining the eremitic way with the life of community, as well as with periodic engagement in apostolic work. Then eremitism developed in Provence, mainly on the islands of Lerin, and in Ireland, Scotland, and Wales. Monks from the British Isles, enchanted by the ideal of "making pilgrimages to God", were going to the Continent in order to establish their hermitages and engage themselves in apostolic activities. The recluses living individually did not practice any liturgical forms of devotion. Except for baptism they did not receive sacraments. According to a common belief of that time, to renounce everything for Christ was the equivalent of a sacrament.

The 11th century brought with it another blossoming of the eremitic life in the West. At that time two eremitic orders were established – the Camaldolese monks in Italy and the Carthusians in France. For their doctrinal basis they looked to the Biblical and patristic tradition and stressed strict solitude and poverty. That was also the moment when severe practices of mortification were being gradually replaced by an eremitism focused more on inner acts. Under the influence of, among others, St.Hildegard of Bingen, continuous wandering started to be seen as not good for the development of the spiritual life. What was now being pointed to was "the inner way" (*itinerarium*) of spiritual growing. It implies the deep sense that all temporal things are fleeting and perishable. Such a perspective makes "a desert" of the monastery and "a departure" (*exodus*) of every personal decision to forsake egoism.

England, Italy, and France saw a number of independent hermits appear there at the turn of the 11th century. They settled in hermitages located in mountains, woods, rock caves, or on islands. A typical forest hermitage was situated in a clearing close to a spring and consisted of a modest hut with a chapel and a moat protecting it against wild animals. Its inhabitant lived by the work of his hands and by alms. The life of those bearded men in string-belted frocks was really modest and simple. Unlike the lifestyle of wealthy abbeys, it did not give any material stability or guarantee any prosperity. These anchorites fell under the jurisdiction of the local bishop or the abbot of their patronal monastery.

Several famous hermits lived and worked in the Slavonic countries. Their life was characterized by great mobility. They were closely connected with aristocratic courts and the Benedictine monasteries as well as keeping in touch with one another. To give some examples, we can list: the Five Polish Brothers, Camaldolese monk-martyrs; Andrew Svorad and Benedict, who lived near the St. Hippolytus abbey in Zabor; and Procopius the Hermit, who established an eremitic community of the Benedictine order in Bohemia.

Eremitism faded away in Germany and Switzerland because of the Reformation, whereas the countries remaining Catholic also at that time witnessed its continuous flowering. The European hermits always lived dispersed and never formed any official provinces to organize themselves as their eastern brothers did. The biggest centers of eremitic life in Europe were found along the French-German border.

In modern times eremitism came back to life in the hermitages established by the St. John the Baptist communities of the Carmelite order. They were located on Vancouver Island and led by Jacques Winandy. The great importance of the eremitic tradition for different Christian denominations, as well as the hermits' contribution to ecumenical unity, was stressed at a symposium of Catholic, Orthodox, and Anglican Churches.

II

A Path Through the Desert

A person does not go to the desert just on a whim, in a moment of melancholy or boredom. But even if that could be the reason, such a trip would end only in a feeling of absurdity and loss. Somebody who is empty cannot stand up to the emptiness of the desert. Somebody who has not discovered the mysterious depth at the very bottom of his own heart cannot discover the mystery of the desert. So, you cannot discover the desert just by chance, just whilst running through your errands. The strict logic of the desert calls for your heart's generosity and your total devotion. Finally, it requires your brave decision to face it to the point of risking your life. Only then may you hear in the vast wilderness the echoing mystery that attracts and scares you, that is at the same time a source of fascination and horror.

1. The Gift of the Eremitic Vocation

The desert, therefore, invites only those who have seen, at the most elementary level of their existence, that they are called to enter the mystery of their own hearts. The mystery's name is love. Anchorites are those who from the very beginning realize that their only chance to understand themselves is to enter into a deep relationship with a loved one. So, why do they want to be alone? Is it not an absurdity?

Towards the mystery

Here we come to a crucial point of the Christian eremitic calling that needs to be explained. For a hermit, the desert is not a god able to serve his private aims, as lofty as they may be. He does not choose his solitude just for its own sake, because in that way he would consciously descend into an abyss. By choosing solitude a Christian takes the side of the mysterious and deep dimension of life which has been revealed in Christ's Cross. And what has been shown in the Cross is the mystery of love of the Trinity, the mystery of forgiveness and mercy. The Cross points to the direction and final aim of the Christian way of life. In any case, the Christian's final destination is a community of love.[2]

Therefore, the stretch of the desert means the stretch of the Cross's arms, the place of self-sacrifice, and the gift of oneself. A spiritually mature person enters the silence and solitude only because he loves and desires to be loved more and more – firstly by God and then by every other human being. The human heart needs solitude and silence because they provide the right perspective for revealing gradually the mystery of life – the mystery of joy and sadness, pain and hope. Solitude turns out to be the path leading us to the truth about God and the truth about ourselves. So there is no trustworthy testimony to the Christian life, there is no authentic friendship, compassion, empathy, or spiritual

---

[2] Cf. *The Constitutions of the Congregation of the Camaldolese Hermits of Monte Corona* (Bloomingdale, Ohio, 1994), pp. 1-2.

openness to love, without the experience of sacred solitude and silence.

These are sacred because they spring from God's heart, sanctified by His holy presence. Eventually silence is the language of love and the prayer arising during the constant experience of the beauty of God's glory. The desert as the land of death, fear, danger, and agony becomes the chosen place for an anchorite. Its meaning has been totally changed from the time of the Biblical Exodus – from that moment it became a place of God's presence, a place of liberation, a meeting place. So the desert may offer not only a mere shelter for all those tired of the humdrum of the cities. The most important thing it offers is a privileged space for contemplation, a distinguished spot where the bright rays of God's glory shine with a special intensity. There in the clear desert sky appears the cloud of presence that leads pilgrims to their final destination.

The rays of love

There are several points of view possible for those who approach the eremitic life. Each of them usually highlights a certain aspect or form of it. The attempts made in that respect by philosophers of religion, sociologists, psychologists, and cultural researchers are often of great value, and nobody should underestimate them. However, the essential sense and direction of the eremitic life may be fully revealed only in the perspective of the gift of the hermit's calling and the specific mission in life that the Father has entrusted to him.

Every human being is a pilgrim in the ways of life. The ways of life exist objectively, because they are concerned with the order of the world and with its ruling principles.

To look for them, to discover and to realize them are the most essential and so the most important goals of human life. Those who set their hearts on responding to their life's calling should be fully aware that their paths are not going to be without difficulties. Just the opposite: every time we try to give a true answer to this gift of life, we may encounter different strains, obstacles, and crises. There is, however, a characteristic trait of a way of life that has been chosen properly. After all the hesitations, defeats, and mistakes, as many as they may be, we can get it together, regain the strength to realize our original goals, and become even more convinced about our life's calling. As a consequence we are rich with the new experience, ready to undertake new efforts, and able to set our goals more precisely.

A great amazement at God's boundless love, revealed in Christ, is the starting point of the eremitic calling. The amazement and wonder are gifts of the Holy Spirit. The Holy Spirit is the Person who inspires the hermit to make the radical choice of abandoning his own plans, worries, and ambitions, the choice of devoting his life to discover the ultimate mystery, which is God.[3] The gift of a calling to follow Christ in a radical way can be realized in many forms. One of them is a very specific or even special form – the calling of a hermit. People who at the bottom of their hearts hear the call to be a hermit know well that for them only life in solitude, poverty, and silence is the best chance to meet God. They realize that among so many possibilities of identifying one's calling, the way of solitude, silence, and inner poverty provides them with the best perspective for finding the lost truth.

---

[3] Cf. ibid., p. 5.

Everyone who discovers in his own soul that specific form of grace that is the charism of the eremitic life sees that the grace is accompanied by a great inner certainty of making the right choice. The certainty and the joy that come along with it stem from finding one's calling in life and mission. The hermit understands more and more that the gift he has received does not belong only to him. On the contrary, the richness of grace is a very concrete call for the anchorite to sacrifice himself for the community of the Church and even for the whole world. The way of the desert is the way of humility and service to every human being, but especially to the most needy and to those lost on the paths of life. And above all it is the service of prayer, sacrifice, renouncement, and mercy that are always powerful and effective. Another dimension of that service may also be achieved thanks to all the different talents and individual strengths for social, organizational, or artistic work that the hermit can employ for the benefit of all in need.

Without a doubt every person has been called to find God, whose glory and splendor prove to be the ultimate in truth, goodness, and beauty. However, there are many different forms and levels of advancement in the journey we undertake to meet the Lord of human history. Many can seek God in their family life and their work for the development of the culture and civilization of the world. For them this kind of engagement is the best way of proving the truth of the Gospel in their own life. But it is not the case for someone called to live as a hermit. When the hermit inspired by the Holy Spirit makes his radical choice and goes away to a desert his goal is clear: he goes there to find total union with God in constant prayer and contemplation.

The particular nature of the charism

The hermit is therefore a very special person, because God has anointed him in an exceptional way, enabling him to cast off all material and spiritual worries. What he focuses on, through prayer and contemplation, is God and God's reign. The hermit, living in the light of God's word, constantly gives himself to prayer, study, meditation, and work in order to bear witness – by means of his own conversion – to the redeeming mission of Christ. This kind of calling needs a great amount of common sense and realism. The hermit gets rid of any illusion of "pure spirituality" and finds his only support in the Cross, which is the central point of God's revelation to humanity. As far as a living faith becomes the power that penetrates every sphere of the anchorite's life, the Risen Lord can act and shine more and more clearly in and through him (2 Cor 3:17-18).

Although the very moment of finding the charism of the eremitic life at the bottom of our heart is decisive, it is only the beginning of the anchorite's journey. Starting from this moment all the following existential experience is going to consist of developing, refining, and appreciating in everyday life the precious gift of this special calling. Only our deep faith can support us in our everyday efforts to understand better and better the importance of our calling and mission. The anchorite is the person obedient to the word that is "a lamp to his feet and a light to his path" [cf. Ps. 118(119): 105]. Only through conscious and obedient faith can the hermit choose and respond to God's grace that has been given him in Christ. Only faith can make him measure up to it, mature, and finally bear the fruit of sanctity.

The hermit is thus ready and able to undertake and carry out many different tasks and duties that are assigned to him in everyday life. He is not in the least a defeatist, a grumbler, or an outsider who does not know how to cope with concrete everyday difficulties and cannot address the problems of life in a responsible way. The hermit makes an effort to live consciously in the world. At the same time though, he appreciates the uniqueness and relevance of the solitude he has chosen. The solitude is his individual and free way of self-determination. By making his choice the hermit turns out to be special in terms of personal growth and development. So what does this process of growth look like?

Usually youth or even childhood is the time of discovering one's life calling. An early delight taken in spending hours alone in the woods, in the mountains, or at a shrine becomes more intense in the course of time. It grows great enough to make us reject the alternative possibilities the world keeps offering to us. The pleasure of aloneness, initially deemed to be just a natural preference, gradually comes under the light of faith and therefore gains a new meaning. From that moment one can see more and more clearly that his life has been put into the perspective of impenetrable mystery. Humility and sincerity of heart are the proper attitudes of someone who waits for the mystery to be revealed.

No doubt a positive response to the gift of the eremitic calling depends on several features of character that enable the person to make such a choice and then to carry it through to completion. After all, the hermit calling is truly unique, it is an exclusive way willingly chosen from a whole range of possibilities. What, therefore, are the traits desirable in someone called to be a hermit?[4]

It seems that those who give a positive answer to the grace of the eremitic life are the people who have reached a proper level of personal maturity in the purely natural sense. Such people develop a positive and realistic self-image reflecting their personal abilities and traits conditioned by their life experience. The sober judgment they display is founded on a sound knowledge of themselves that is free from any affectation and illusion. One cannot arrive at a clear and coherent view of reality without a kind of inner discipline, an ability to control and direct one's own emotions, thoughts, and drives. In this sense self-control is a personal ability to coordinate all levels of the human personality with a conscious, faith-motivated choice of values.

The hermit comes to a realistic and objective judgment of himself quite spontaneously. His courageous openness towards reality in terms of culture, social and political conditions, religion, and spirituality bears fruit in the form of his personal authenticity. Taking into account the whole context of reality is possible only because the hermit tends to perceive the world with the "eyes of the heart". As a matter of fact he wants to ponder over many different subjects and problems and does not limit his reflection just to the sphere of religion in its narrow sense. Thanks to his sound personal, social, and religious formation the hermit can see the ongoing problems of the world in several dimensions, considering their philosophical, sociological, political, and moral meaning. But that is not all.

---

[4] Cf. K. Osińska, *Pustelnicy dziś* (Warsaw, 1988), pp. 41ff.

In order to attain a realistic judgment of his own situation the hermit has to put it against an historical and global background. Having realized that his individual life is nourished by the general human culture achieved throughout the ages, the hermit tries to learn about, understand, and appreciate this heritage. The hermit's way thus has nothing to do with running away from the world and everyday difficulties. Just the opposite, it is a deep appreciation and concern for the world and its problems. This is the appreciation and concern that stem from love and compassion. The hermit, therefore, is a person who is active in numerous fields, shows many interests, enjoys life, and often has a great sense of humor.

The hermit may also be characterized by another feature: a significant independence in his opinions, activities, and decisions. Such independence does not result from the passing whims of an unbalanced personality, from an excessive individualism or pride. The anchorite fosters a deep concern for social matters. Spontaneously he is eager to help wherever a pain can be eased, poverty can be lessened, or human rights and dignity need to be guarded. So, the hermit's consistency and independence of action do not bear the stamp of haughtiness, vehemence, or stubbornness. They rather flow out of a heart that is strong, recollected, and also humble.

The personal independence of the hermit can be seen clearly in how unaffected he is by the pressure of surrounding opinions. Walking on his difficult and even dangerous path, he must be almost naturally adept at determining his own opinion, forming his own independent judgment, and taking on new and unconventional perspectives. After all he is free from the burden of public opinion and so able, in a wise and simple way, to resist all popular views that are often oversimplified, superficial, or even cheap and vulgar.

In fact, just by the very nature of his calling the hermit is "somehow different". It is interesting that everyone who meets him can sense that "difference" instantly. He is not different, though, as an old bachelor, a crank with complexes, might be different. The hermit's peculiarity is rooted rather in his mature, extraordinary, and strong personality that amazes and attracts others because it is sincere, deep, and simple.

Without a doubt each authentic anchorite is a kind of sage for those who seek his help and support. His wisdom strikes a harmony between ideals and life; he lives what he preaches. Also his practical knowledge, based on many years of experience, does him credit. So the different character of the hermit does not imply an alienation or remoteness. He is "different" because he lives his calling in a spontaneous and authentic way, because he indeed believes in truth, justice, and peace. His paths, way of thinking, and choices, particular as they are, positively radiate a special warmth and charm wherever he goes.

The possibility of faith

The features described above are only a rough sketch of the hermit's character. It is obvious that not everyone whose natural attributes match these characteristics would decide to choose the life of solitude. On the other hand, the eremitic life often attracts those who, at the beginning of the way, lack many of the essential features needed to be a hermit. However, thanks to God's grace and due to their own determination and efforts, they can achieve such a level of personal development that subsequently they become hermits of high caliber.

Of course, faith should be the decisive factor in entering upon the Christian eremitic life. Faith is also the most important element determining the ultimate direction and character of the hermit's way of life. Here we have to stress the faith factor strongly, because there are many cases where a quite non-religious motivation underlies the decision for the eremitic life. Often people choose the life of solitude because of some ideas of charity they foster, as a kind of social service they intend to undertake or as their engagement in some ecological movement. We can tell by experience that those merely natural motivations can be strong and mature enough to successfully inspire a person to live as a hermit.

In fact, the life of every hermit should be measured both by the dimension of his service to others and by the dimension of his openness towards the world and its needs. But this service may be limited to the perspective of our earthly existence and never be able to overcome such a limitation; or, on the contrary, it may be the expression of our faith in God and thus able to reach eternity.[5]

For hermits concentrated on charity, the love of neighbor is the essence of their life calling. Their commitment often means more than helping others to solve material or health problems. For humanitarian reasons they engage also in concrete actions defending human rights and dignity. In so doing, they do not worry about branching off from their charism of the eremitic life, because the solitude they have chosen is the solitude of serving all the needy. So they try to be active and creative in all different fields as intellectuals, writers, editors, ecologists, or foresters. With their zeal

---

[5] Cf. K. Osińska, op. cit., p. 152.

and openness they place themselves at the front line of the struggle for the better future of humanity.

The hermits devoted to social service have clean hands. They can be characterized by modesty, a sense of proportion, discretion, creativity, and unselfishness. Whatever they do is always a kind of testimony to the values they believe in, and that is why their activity has such a powerful impact. Active in different organizations and communities, they make efforts to see the problems they deal with as objectively as possible. Intuitively they know how to choose the right solution even when it seems impossible to find one.

Undoubtedly, that merely humanitarian aspect of the hermit's calling and engagement has great value and brightens up the everyday life of communities. However, it is not that kind of calling that is going to be the subject of this book. Here, we rather want to examine, at least to a certain extent, the way of life in which a person follows the poor, abandoned, and lonely Christ and does so in a spirit of faith, solitude, and silence. These are the basic and characteristic means for discovering the mystery of God, humanity, and the world. So in this book we would like to present the Christian way of life in solitude, a way that is accepted as a gift from the hands of our Lord and Creator.

The Christian anchorite goes to the desert in order to find freedom and peace. By renouncing any vanity, ambition, rivalry, and success, he makes efforts to concentrate all of his spiritual powers on the ultimate mystery that bit by bit reveals itself before his eyes. In other words the anchorite is a person who decides, in solitude and silence, to protect and cultivate the seed of the Gospel. It is the experience of a living faith that determines his way of life. Such a person is formed by being meek and obedient to the delicate inspirations of the Holy Spirit, who opens up the paths to meeting things infinite and eternal. The hermit is immersed in a search for God without awareness of an onset or a term, and so he abandons his direct activity in the world and can more fully entrust himself to redeeming Providence.

To search for God means, above all, to enter the way of faith and silence that releases the spring of prayer at the bottom of the human heart. The space of silence is gradually being filled with prayer, which is, at the same time, a gift and the greatest task and commitment in the hermit's life. The silence of God Himself, which is a song of love, starts to ring out in the inner room of the poor and lonely soul. When the hermit finds this marvelous silence in his own heart, he can find it also in the hearts of the people he meets. In this way of life every moment is transformed by the refreshing streams of prayer. The hermit who looks for the Lord in the solitude of his own heart and mind will be, sooner or later, filled abundantly with the Lord's silent word. Thanks to this he will be able to understand unmistakably the plans of Providence. God reveals Himself to a person as lightning against the sky of the poor human heart, a flash that for a moment lights up the heart's mysterious depths. In these moments the lonely voyager suddenly knows eternity present in the midst of time.

2. The Gift of Solitude

How can we speak about the eremitic calling at a moment when common human solidarity, community, or just simply "being together" are taken as "signs of the times"? Is it not the case that people today understand solitude only in a negative sense, as a synonym for emptiness, failure, danger, and other adversities? Is it not the case that the situation of "being lonely" seems to be the most tragic possibility for people of modern times, the possibility that causes fear and a sense of total infirmity?[6]

Solitude of the heart

The hermit feels that he is called to enter solitude both in its external and internal sense. In an elementary individual experience the hermit encounters the solitude of his own heart, the solitude of his own existence that makes him a unique human being. This basic experience of meeting one's own situation of existence that is prior to any human relationship has, for a lonely human being, a decisive meaning: it shapes his future way of life. A wise recognition of the limitations, as well as the horizons, of one's own existence is the condition of each successful human relationship. As a matter of fact these two perspectives merge with each other and are mutually related. One cannot recognize and understand the meaning of one's own solitude without meeting other people, also lonely in their existence. In the face of the other man we can see every feature of our own, the other face reveals ours to us.

Solitude, which paradoxically we happen to notice most intensely when we relate to another "thou", is a fertile soil in which grows our authentic life's calling of solitude by choice. Only the one who is fully aware of the great value of human relationships, bonds, and connections can decide on giving

---

[6] Cf. M.Zawada, *Zaślubiny z samotnością* (Cracow, 1999), pp. 109ff.

them up to God in order to find them anew in an even fuller way. So, the choice of the eremitic calling should be made in freedom and humility. The person who is called to remain alone and makes his independent choice for solitude is, above all, a herald of the absolutely precious and meaningful love that is continuously going on in the depths of the triune God. By his withdrawal from the world, the hermit wants to manifest the eternal dimension in every moment of his own life and, in some way, to make eternity present here and now. That is why the eremitic way of life, properly understood and experienced, is not only based on natural character but is also given as a gift that enables one to find and recover one's own existence in God.

To be a hermit means to relate to the mystery that is present in every human life and that makes one feel small and powerless. To see with the eyes of faith the marvelous and eternal beauty of God means to be invited to come out of oneself and to give oneself up to God. Therefore, the only possible life option that makes sense for the hermit is to become fully open to that absolute perspective of giving himself as a gift to God. In this sense, the eremitic calling is a consequence of meeting the original depths of the Trinity's solitude. God is the living interpersonal relationship of love inasmuch as He is the presence of the original abyss of solitude and silence. The reality of God is thus the original source of any solitude, an impenetrable abyss that calls to the profound depths of solitude of the human heart. Having heard that existential call of God's solitude, people respond to it by opening up the whole secret of their hearts.[7]

---

[7] Cf. Louis Dupré, *The Interior Life: The Origins of Trinitarian Mysticism and its Development by Jan Ruusbroec;* quoted after L. Dupré, Głębsze życie (Cracow, 1994), pp. 91ff.

So for the hermit, to choose solitude means to give his faith's consent to stand by the God who calls him. Such a choice is the expression of an inner desire to give oneself up to God who is calling by the gift of His overwhelming presence. The original revelation of the beauty of God's face inspires one to renounce everything, including personal participation in the human community, and to devote the rest of one's life to seeking and contemplating God's magnificence. The hermit's solitude imprints a special brand on his whole existence and becomes for him a basic perspective for meeting God. The ways we approach the mystery of God, as well as the way we perceive it, come from a simple experience of faith. Therefore, to meet the absolute mystery never means to understand it completely. Such an experience always leaves us surprised, astounded, and longing to be united with that original beauty.

For the hermit, solitude has its own structure, its inner logic, and, last but not least, its hidden wisdom. Solitude cannot be overlooked as unimportant, because it is a crucial element of the hermit's experience. A person who searches for it and subsequently experiences the power of its tranquility becomes enchanted with the charm of seclusion. It is just the solitude that constitutes the special everyday atmosphere of the hermit's life, this unique environment to kindle a flame of intense prayer springing from the love of God. And this is the most exclusive love of all, demanding a person's total devotion. The flame of God's love penetrates through the hermit's whole life, changing and bringing light to all the aspects of his existence. In other words, every single element of the hermit's life is lit up by the rays of God's presence. This does not mean that it is enough for the hermit to be close to his Lord without making any sacrifices or mortifications. On the contrary, the love that has been ignited in the human heart can burn and grow only in those who enliven their souls with mortification and penance.

The solitude of encounter

In fact, the hermit who is called to live in solitude is never lonely. This situation stems from a basic paradox of the eremitic calling. One called to live in solitude is at the same time invited to associate with God. Such a person's existence is characterized by a constant effort to follow Christ. Our Heavenly Father leads us out into the desert so He can nourish us, as He nourished Christ Himself, only with the food of His mercy. The hermit knows well the taste of the Lord's mercy, because it is the only source of strength that supports him in his material and spiritual poverty. To know the Lord's mercy is, in practice, to trust in His grace and generosity. The anchorite is able to find himself only if he comes out of himself and entrusts to God everything that he is or may become.

So, the hermit's solitude is the key to the door of the mystery of his own heart. The only possible way of revealing the mystery is the way of service that is one with love of God and the world. Acting in harmony with the Holy Spirit, the hermit realizes that his own existence is rooted in the silent presence of his Maker. A great spiritual effort together with an inner chastity and renunciation are needed to maintain such a spiritual awareness. On the other hand, however, the hermit learns that he can reach the fullness of his spiritual life only by accepting calmly the gift of grace and by letting

God do His great work in the human heart. Ultimately, the existential solitude of the hermit can be understood and accepted only in relation to the original solitude of God Himself.

The taste of the hermit's solitude is the taste of prayer, a flavor of the constant effort to meet the Absolute. Our heart's freedom that comes to life in the desert results from our longing to be close to the Father and from our desire for His predilection. This is the freedom springing from a simple, supernatural love, which sets us free from ourselves and enables us to come face to face with our solitude. This love can also be described as a kind of communion with the absolute Freedom that is totally unconditional and unrestrained. The eremitic calling comes to its fullness in humble thanksgiving and adoration. Then the basic, or rather the only thing that our hearts need worry about is how to give way and let God wrap us in His loving and compassionate care.

The hermit entrusts himself to God's care in a specific way: his solitary life is always full of gratitude towards God and towards all people. He is the person who has become humble and silent enough to understand and enjoy the goodness visible in the whole of creation. The goodness reflects the beauty of the Father and is a clear evidence of His goodness, easily recognized by a simple and grateful heart. The hermit, led by the wisdom of the Holy Spirit, follows the Spirit's inspiration and tries to make his whole human life reflect the glory of God. What he boasts of is the original beauty of his Lord. Moreover, he himself becomes a sign of God's blessing to the world. For such a person to be a blessing to creation means to a certain extent to be a reflection of the rays of God's beauty, to be the glory of God.

Therefore, spiritual solitude cannot be in any way a lasting burden of suffering, torment, or confusion. Besides, by entering his extraordinary way in the spirit of freedom and renunciation, the hermit becomes an example and a tower of strength for all those who painfully experience inner loneliness while living among other people in society. Everyone who makes the free choice to fulfill his life's calling in solitude should be ready to become, sooner or later, a friend to the great many of those lost and lonely who will turn to him for support and spiritual comfort.

The solitude of service

To experience solitude is to meet a fullness of life that calls to be shared with every other person. The hermit is aware of his responsibility for the world. As he is able to discern the things that are important, he can be free from any kind of convention or routine in his evaluations. Nothing can be more distant from the spiritual approach of the hermit than an attitude of isolation, insularity, or fundamentalism. His broad-mindedness and the sobriety of his judgments stem from his meeting with God, which is for him the source of both his simplicity and deep spirituality. For others sometimes it is difficult to accept and understand the hermit's innovative and fresh approach towards the world and people. His original opinions often stir up opposition, even enmity, against him. To be able to keep faith with himself and his calling, the hermit needs the spiritual power that is fortitude. This is the virtue that guards him against drifting with the tide of banality and everyday commercialism. This is the virtue that also guards his persistence and fidelity to the way of life he has chosen once and for all, a way that is often spiced with bitterness.

When a person chooses solitude as a sure way of meeting God, he not only gains the great chance of attaining the full development of his personality and a proper understanding of his individual dignity. Such a person can also become a concrete and very special gift for his Church and community. One cannot bring any joy, cheerfulness, or optimism into a community unless he knows well the value of his own person and unless he fully appreciates it. At the same time, solitude gives one a sense of personal weakness, imperfection, and fallibility. This sense is one of the most important factors in the process of the purification of the heart. The spirit of pride, haughtiness, complacency, and hypocrisy is always a danger for the hermit. Seeing one's own weakness and existential poverty can be a turning point towards taking a more realistic view of the spiritual life. In this way weakness becomes the source of evangelical might, and poverty and humility become the conditions for acknowledging the truth about oneself and the world. Solitude, by means of making an individual face the naked truth, sets him free from the past and the future, from the world of men and events. This is how Kierkegaard wrote of it, beautifully employing the tension of paradox:

> Alone by himself he stands in the wide world.
> He has no contemporary time to support him;
> he has no past to long for, since his past has not
> yet come; he has no future to hope for, since
> his future is already past. Alone, he has the
> whole world over against him as the other with
> which he finds himself in conflict; for the rest

of the world is to him only one person, and this
person, this inseparable, importunate friend, is
Misunderstanding. He cannot become old, for he
has never been young; he cannot become young,
for he is already old. In one sense of the word he
cannot die, for he has not really lived; in another
sense he cannot live, for he is already dead.[8]

The ties of friendships the hermit makes in the course of
time light up his solitude. Paradoxically, the hermit, by leaving
the human community, "establishes" a new community of
faithful friends, who "gather around" him. These are usually
people whom he once helped, friends loyal till death. Making
friends with persons of the opposite sex and retaining
complete chastity is a rare ability, which hermits often have.
What characterize their friendships are mutual devotion,
faithfulness, and complete unselfishness.

The solitude of death

The solitude of the desert teaches a person to be at
peace even in the face of death. The hermit sees everything
through a child's eyes and heart. Since he is not attached
to any popular views or widespread opinions, his solitude
becomes a foretaste of eternity. The holy time of liturgy, the
time of embracing past, present, and future things, is his
time. The hermit does not meet eternity in the way gnostics
are tempted to meet it. He does not reject what is temporal.
He has his share of eternity by raising all earthly things up to
their ultimate fullness by virtue of Christ's redemptive love.

---

[8] Søren Kierkegaard, *Either/Or* (Princeton, New Jersey, 1971), vol. 1, p.
224.

This gives him an inner peace, which helps to overcome the fear of death.

The mere choice of solitude is an experience of *kenosis* and death. The hermit, with his childlike heart, approaches death fearlessly. He accepts it with quiet understanding and patience. He does not try to avoid death, to run away from it, or to forget the inevitable necessity of dying. It is simply because his practice of the eremitic life has awakened in him a deep sense of the fact that life and death, as people call them, are constantly alternating with each other. The hermit is perfectly aware that after each inhalation there comes an exhalation, after a sunrise a sunset, after a blossoming a withering. He knows well that what we call "death" is a necessary component of the process called "life". It is obvious for him that he is not going to bear fruit in his life unless he dies. As a person touching death at every moment of his life, he accepts the necessity of ending his earthly pilgrimage in peace and serenity because he remembers that his death has been transformed by the power of the Resurrection. The way in which he arrives at such understanding is not just by pondering the principles of life, but by standing firm in the realm of death with his whole existence.

A special dimension of joy, springing from what we can call for short "the wisdom of life", permeates the hermit's solitude. Of course, the harmony and simplicity that accompany the hermit in everyday life do not shield him from experiencing pain and suffering. The very decision for the solitary life in service to God and specific people involves the danger of being deeply hurt and the possibility of experiencing various torments. To remain bravely and persistently within the limits of one's cell means to accept defeats, personal crises, and temptations of losing the chosen way of life. It means to give one's consent to all those difficult moments that can crush even the strong. But such an acceptance has nothing to do with resignation or passive approval for whatever blind fate may bring. The hermit's faith and prayer enable him to gradually transform his pain into a creative form of love. How is this possible?

Solitude is for the hermit not only a natural environment of life but, most of all, it is a supernatural value. It is because the hermit's solitude makes him participate a little bit in Christ's Cross. The hermit, following in the bloody steps of his Master, is going to struggle – in solitude and with inner disturbances – against the evil present in the world. In this way the hermit's solitude takes the form of silent martyrdom and becomes a personal sacrifice of himself. For the hermit, these difficult periods of suffering are not only the path towards his own sanctity. But also, by touching the dark side of existence, the hermit strives for a blessing for all humanity. We have to remember that the calling to solitude is a special charism in service to the Church and the whole world. And this is another reason why the hermit's solitude does not mean loneliness, but just the opposite: the hermit knows that he is close to the whole world in joy, suffering, death, and resurrection.

So, the hermit's solitude is a real gift for the community of the Church and for the whole world. The elementary motive for choosing this extraordinary way of life is adoration of God, who is worthy of all glory, and seeking the good of all men. The hermit enters his specific way of salvation, the way that radiates widely with its testimony, by identifying himself with Christ's sacrifice and by yearning for communion with the mystery of Christ's life. By dying in Christ and rising in Christ, touching the mystery of Christ's Passover, the hermit becomes a prophet sent to the people of today.

Despite all the difficulties and hardships of his way, the hermit should not be afraid of his own solitude. In the course of time he will be able to see more and more clearly the final aim and the ultimate meaning of his life's calling. The act of casting aside all fears and personal worries may be even a kind of penance – the penance of entrusting those aspects of our human weakness to Christ. Christ is, above all, the One who entered the horror of utmost suffering, experienced the most painful loneliness, and yet overcame them with the power of His trust placed in the Father. It is not so seldom that the hermit weeps over a sufferer. This is the gift of tears, that touches the very center of his heart, and this is a special moment when Christ Himself weeps with us and in us. So acts the Holy Spirit, whose gift opens the cleansing and refreshing spring of tears. The hermit does not try to analyze or search for reasons for the tears; he rather trusts that in them Christ washes away all the guilt of the degraded world.

3. The Gift of Silence

The hermit, called to live in poverty and solitude, walks off into the desert in order to seek and find his beloved Lord there. But in fact what is the starting point of this "seeking the Lord"? What does "seeking the Lord" mean for a person who has entrusted the whole future to God, to God who is calling?[9]

---

[9] Cf. M. Zawada, op.cit., pp. 25ff.

The silence that listens intently

The hermit's openness towards God's calling is based on self-renunciation and rejecting personal opinions, views, and dreams. It is based on entering the dimension of silence. However, the hermit has nothing in common with the deserter who runs away from the truth, too weak to be its faithful witness. The hermit leaves his own likes and hopes, but he does so in a positive way. He is not at all a slave, with a heart shrinking with loss, helplessness, horror, and despair. Undoubtedly the hermit's way is marked by a number of paradoxes, dramas, and crises. But surely it is not, in the slightest sense, the way of absurdity and tragedy that might characterize a fruitless existence, an existence stripped of any eternal meaning.

The hermit's attitude of self-abandonment, related deeply to the realm of silence, reveals his faith and love. This self-abandonment contains both an element of spiritual dying and an element of being born to a new life of grace. The hermit's openness is simply the attitude of faith, which means rejecting all the deceitful half-truths offered by the world. Faith means also standing by the Truth revealed in the Son of God. The hermit, as one who is faithful, listens to the Word. To listen to the Word is firstly to be obedient to it *(ob-audire)**. Here, the disposition of faith includes caring for things that are eternal, so from its very beginning it is immersed in the atmosphere of the Spirit. That is why in the eyes of the hermit something can be important and valuable only as far as it breathes the air of eternity.

---

* Translator's note: In Polish, "posłuszny" (obedient) is derived from "słuchać" (to listen).

For the hermit, faith is a special covenant with God. By it, he chooses to commit himself with full confidence in God's unlimited freedom. The act of entrustment, risky as it may be, is also an act of special responsibility. At this moment the hermit agrees that caring and striving for the kingdom of God will be his only true task and duty in life. The hermit looks carefully with the eyes of faith at the Incarnate Word and tries to fathom the mystery of His divine mission. Christ, the Incarnate Covenant, is the One in whom the hermit wants to recognize the unique aspect of his personal calling and mission.

Basically, silence is a person's strictly defined stance in relation to the revelation of the Word, the stance referred to above as "faith". Faith characterizes, illustrates, and expresses this special space of silence, which is much deeper and much more basic than a mere absence of words. It is not only because faith, as the act of listening, necessarily requires the hermit to keep silent. Here the reason for silence is much more essential: it goes down to the foundations of existence because it takes its origin from God. The Father pronounces His Word in the most elementary silence of His divinity. The silence of the triune God provides the hermit's life with a unique perspective. It sheds light so that the hermit can come closer to the essence of the human and material world. That is why being introduced to this new dimension of silence means making one of the basic conscious choices that will enable the hermit to experience fully his way of life.

The silence of adoration

The hermit, therefore, chooses to remain silent because he has revived an elementary human desire to listen to God's word. The word is an abundant fullness that lights up what is hidden in darkness. When it appears on the horizon of our life, it invites us to a meeting and to a pure and simple dialogue of faith. This appearance of God is so unusual and overwhelming that we respond to it at first with a deep astonishment, awe, and adoration. The Lord who passes by makes us bashful with the splendor of His glory. Our bashfulness is the most elementary and the most suitable response a human heart can have in the presence of God. God, going out to meet the hermit, finds him waiting, concentrated and silent.

So, the hermit's silence has nothing to do with a merely natural emptiness, a lack of words, or an absence of thoughts. No, just the opposite. This silence is always and from the depths of its source a sound of Silence, the fullness of God's presence that speaks the language of the triune God. The hermit cannot become a slave of mortification, because any mortification he undertakes, he does so simply for the sake of meeting the living God. The gift of love "requires" an answer. The answer, being the most beautiful kind of human love, is at the same time the path of the most creative form of mortification. That is why the hermit's way is so amazingly dynamic and fruitful – a way characterized by a radical attitude of being stripped of all unnecessary things, including the burden of unnecessary words.

The hermit is therefore a person who waits in silence and who opens his heart to the gift of a new time and a new history. When he in the humbleness of his faith listens to the Word, he gradually gains access to what is eternal. When he opens the eyes of his pure heart to the flash of God's glory, he experiences a synthesis, the whole of reality centered around the axis of the Word. Thus the silence seems to be a steadfast presence before things that are eternal, a presence that is full of trust and patience. It becomes the most clear and distinct expression of human freedom. The hermit's freedom expresses itself in a humble and respectful disposition towards the mystery of the Word, which is ever being revealed anew. Freedom is possible only due to a fond hope that the realm of the last things (Greek: *ta eschata*) is going to come, the hope that the Covenant's promise is going to be kept. Faith put in the perspective of the ultimate goal, dynamic as it is, makes it possible to cover all unimportant and banal things with a mantle of silence.

Basically, the hermit's silence is not a mere absence of words. In spite of a great need for communication, humans are silent beings by nature because they emerged from the eternal silence of God who created them in His own image. Silence can liberate us from the pressure of knowledge and information, from the crowd of words. Today especially it can be a very precious way to protest against all the situations when language is misused, trivialized, falsified, or made irrelevant. The power of silence gives a new value, a new structure, and a new meaning to the word; it is not too much to say that through silence the word can find its original sanctity.

The silence of presence

The *Logos* that is being pronounced in the womb of God's silence is holy of itself. People who in their religious and existential experience touch this original sphere of silence become themselves a reflection of God's sanctity. The sphere of *sacrum* gives space for a specific synthesis of body and spirit, light and darkness, word and silence. This is the place where the essence of the hermit's life and the essence of his words reach accord and harmony in a really unique way: in a sense, a person who is holy can make the Word of God present. So we can say that the hermit's life and words are not only a sign denoting another dimension of reality, but they are also a realization of God's presence in the world. That is why the hermit is called ultimately not to keep an absolute silence, but to pronounce the word that carries a flash of God's wisdom. The hermit's ministry for the community of the Church takes the form of a "sacrament", and his life resounds with the mystery. His life is the moment when the mystery of God's salvation reveals itself, more or less directly, in a world of pain and fear. Silence, giving birth to words that are inspired and meaningful, becomes the stimulus and the source of creative power, which can change our lives.

Silence for the hermit is first a presence and second a meeting. Through silence we are given access to the mystery of our own lives, the mystery of their beauty and simplicity. Through silence we are taught how to relate to the depths of our own selves and, gradually and sometimes after long efforts, how to return to the inmost center of our own person, which is the place where we can commune with God in the fullest and truest way. So silence is a real though immeasurable energy, a flash of truth, eternity, and God's mystery. This is how silence, seemingly empty, reveals its meaning: the Presence, which as openness seeks fulfillment in the Meeting. Love as the Meeting avoids too many words, images, and symbols. Its power can be visible in participation – union, which is full of awe and wonder and rejects everything that is insipid and trivial.

Silence, the hermit's basic disposition of faith towards God, becomes for him the simplest way to discover the truth. It is a divine principle ruling in the human heart that makes it possible for us to draw closer to the most important truths of life. At the same time, silence is able to bring to light any falsehood or lie. A marvelous quality of silence opens up and reveals the true meaning held captive in every form, and thus it encompasses all forms. Silence, the shape of all shapes, is an expression of eternal things. Its structure displays an ultimate kind of form that is able to radiate from its very center the light of truth. Silence thus can be meaningful only for those who sense and understand its specific language and logic.

The transparency and openness of the silent presence reveals also an amazing and a totally new quality of human perception. The silence is only seemingly amorphous. In fact it is not groundless to point out its specific logic or even its specific structure. Silence, the original environment of life and love, is a unique bridge connecting the human heart with the essence of the truth, the truth that manifests itself as splendor and astonishing beauty. So, it is no wonder that one of the basic conditions of aesthetic perception consists of silence. A solitary who practices silence is gradually being enabled to perceive the supernatural Beauty that has been revealed in Christ. The magnificence of His glory manifested on the Mount of Transfiguration, and paradoxically even more clearly on Calvary, is easily recognized by those who through their practice of silence know how to look at reality not in a pragmatic way, but in the esthetic way of faith.

4. Seeking God

The gift of a calling to the life of solitude, silence, fasting, and prayer is the way in which the hermit seeks the Lord.[10] All other possible goals of the hermit's life yield to this one and prevailing desire of his soul. Nobody goes to the desert in order to look for prestige, acceptance, success, or fame. Such reasons would quickly lead to madness or demonic possession. Going out to the desert makes sense only for people who are free, to a considerable extent, from the pressure of pride and egoism. If this is not the case, and there is another reason for choosing solitude other than God's grace, God's gift of love, then the person will quit the chosen way quickly or fall into an abyss of despair and madness.

The desire of meeting

The hermit does not want to look out for his own interest, he does not aim at acquiring any material possessions, and moreover he is also free from the desire of gathering any spiritual goods. At the beginning of his way the hermit may be influenced by different fascinations or worries that still dwell in his heart. However, in the course of his spiritual progress, sooner or later, he comes to the conviction that he has no desires or wishes. What he is completely concentrated

---

[10] Cf. Thomas Merton, *The Silent Life* (New York, 1961), p. 9.

on is not his search for something, but his search for Someone. People who live in solitude are sincere and simple seekers of revealed truth, which has a fully personal character because it is the unity of the Divine Persons. All other aspects of the hermit's everyday life are not so much submitted to this basic search as resultant from it. What motivates every action of the hermit is the desire for love. Through it the hermit hopes to find the lost beauty of God's glory. Entering the space of solitude and silence he paradoxically focuses on meeting and dialogue with God and with the human other. Here is how J. Tischner comments on the reality of this meeting:

> To meet somebody means to experience the person's face. Experiencing the other's face reveals his truth. What is necessary to make the meeting happen is mutuality; if we want to see the other person's face, we have to uncover our own face, and the other must have the intention to accept what has been revealed. . . . The meeting of persons is so persuasive that it is able to change radically one's attitude towards the world around us, to form anew one's lifestyle in this world, to challenge the hierarchy of values so far accepted. The meeting introduces us to the depths of all the mysteries of existence, where questions about the sense and nonsense of everything are born.[11]

So seeking God in the way of the desert will not be creative, will not build up the personality of the hermit or the community he wants to serve and strengthen, unless

---

[11] J. Tischner, "Bezdroża spotkań", in *Analecta Cracoviensia* (Cracow, 1980), vol. XII, pp. 137, 142.

his spiritual efforts focus on attaining communion with the triune God. A person can meet another and enter into a positive relationship with the other only by means of a dialogue. Getting to know and love the other's innermost being is possible only through the trustful and humble attitude of one's "I" towards the other's "thou". This relationship also illustrates, by analogy, the mystery of God. God is not only omnipotent and omniscient. God's very nature consists of being the loving community of the Persons of the Trinity. The beauty of this love is shed on the whole created world. A person of faith not only wants to follow in the world the footsteps of his beloved Lord. The believer longs for a meeting with God, the source and the ultimate meaning of every created thing, for a meeting with the One who is personal love.

What thus always precedes the eremitic calling is the burning desire to attain communion with Christ, a spiritual ardor that dominates all aspects of life. This longing and anxiety have been initiated by God's personal revelation through the gift of the Word. The Word that has been truly heard once and then understood is an impulse that awakens the human spirit from its torpor, and it is an invitation to a meeting. Christ demands our response to be still fuller and more truthful. He waits for our answer, which eventually should be the gift of love. As soon as one hears the voice ringing in the wilderness, he gets up at night like the bride in the Song of Songs and starts seeking the One for whom his soul is longing. The hermit's answer to the call is, from the very beginning, an active search for the One who is calling. It engages his all: the body, mind, and heart. The search that the hermit undertakes does not aim at a singular material or spiritual object. All things are encompassed by the overflow of his heart, wounded and captured by the onslaught of God's love.

Here we have a clear answer to the question of how it is possible to leave everything and to enter the realm of solitude by virtue of the gift of God's kingdom present in the grace of the eremitic calling. God's calling is sweet, but at the same time it allows for no objection or delay. The grace of the eremitic calling is like a rapid river, which floods the human heart so powerfully that it is simply impossible not to abandon everything and meet the One who is calling. However, the need to abandon oneself and to go out to meet the Presence that opens up as a gift is in no way a pre-determination. Although we may speak of "the need", this only means the necessity of loving, which makes one restless unless he finds a dwelling in a community of love.

Obviously the process of going out to meet the calling Presence has no beginning and no end. That is because it takes its source from the everlasting dynamism of God's life. By answering the call, one takes a step on the way of entrance into the everlasting dialogue that takes place in God's very bosom. The dialectics of listening and responding marks the eremitic way from its very beginning. Every word that has been heard ignites our desire to make a gift and a sacrifice. It thus liberates us from ourselves and enables us to open our heart to the rays of the truth. Consequently, through this inner openness and spiritual sensibility, we become even more attentive and eager to listen and understand the calling voice of everlasting love, the love that waits for our human "yes" to be said anew again and again.

The Word who calls wants our hearts to be undivided and totally dedicated. That is why we need to abandon everything, to remove ourselves from everything in order to come to full communion. If we failed to respond, we would bring about our spiritual death, because the joy of listening to and answering the grace of the Word is the very life of the hermit. When we listen intently and respond actively in faith, our desire for silence, solitude, and inner concentration grows even more. The hermit never ceases to enjoy the gift of his calling, the gift that turns every day into a feast day.

In the shadow of the Cross

But the hermit's days are not free from tears, pain, and sadness. Just the opposite – tribulation remains present in the way of the eremitic pilgrimage. The Word that we respond to, however, is the One who has created us and who is constantly renewing our youth with His love. So to encounter the pain of our existence is to get another impulse to search, to listen, and to respond even more actively and faithfully. In this way we can be motivated to open ourselves up even more to the radiating Presence of the Lord, whose glory is fully revealed in the shadow of the Cross. The voice that calls and the answer that we give never separate us from the refreshing air of this space. In fact, the fullness of the eremitic life is nothing else but the contemplation of God's magnificence that flashes at the intersection of the bars of the Cross. Any other perspective must be incomplete or even false.

The eremitic calling therefore pertains to the reality that the Church calls the contemplative life. Its essence consists in the ongoing effort of faith, which through prayer and the sacraments seeks lasting communion with the God who is still calling. Eremitic contemplation has nothing to do with mere passivity or spiritual stagnation. Rather, it is vital and intent listening and attentive gazing, with the eyes of faith, at the glory of the approaching Word that becomes the one and only desire of the human heart. Contemplation therefore refers to a faith so strong that it focuses all one's spiritual efforts on the search for God. The search for God, with its inner dynamism, has no end, because it refers to things that are absolute and unconditional.[12]

The hermit finds his Lord in prayer, in the sacraments, and in the word of Scripture. Here however he encounters a paradox: at the very moment he becomes convinced that he has reached the Object of his efforts and desires, he sees that such an accomplishment is completely impossible. When all is said and done, to find God means to seek Him continuously and unceasingly, because in fact what is searched for is not a thing that has been lost, but a personal Mystery that offers itself as a gift of love. To discover the mystery of Christ means to realize that it cannot be grasped or comprehended fully. Here our thirst will never be satisfied completely. What we can do is to admire and adore the absolute Mystery that reveals itself before the eyes of faith. So in this basic sense we can love it. The hermit's way is the way of adoring the truth that he met, which he touches and to which he bears witness, even if he is not always fully aware of doing so.

The search for God may take a twofold form. The person who is aware of God's transcendence cannot find Him in the world of people and things. God is infinitely "other" from

---

[12] Cf. L. Bouyer, *Le sens de la vie monastique* (Paris, 1962), p. 14.

anything that the human heart can comprehend or touch. At the same time, however, God is the openness of love that sheds its abundant goodness over the whole universe. This paradox imprints a special brand on the hermit's and every Christian's way of salvation. When we make an effort to return to the Father's house we meet, above all, the dazzling mystery of His glory. God dwells in inaccessible light and His face is veiled with an unfathomable brightness that guards the mystery of absolute and inner beauty. At the same time the magnificence of God's glory is present and manifest in the Church where, thanks to the mission of the Son and the descent of the Spirit, everyone has access to the Father. Walking carefully along the path of apparent contradictions and tensions, the hermit learns how to look for and find God whom his whole soul and body are yearning for. Without the Father's generous openness to the world in the mission of Christ, He would have been completely inaccessible to us.

Another person's mystery can be recognized only in a personal dialogue that "reveals the face" of the other. The mutual openness, presence, relationship, and dialogue are an actual place for the revelation of the other person's face. Seeking and fathoming God is similar. It is in our human hearts, always open to God's actual grace, where the Word reveals itself, but it is never our human merit that initiates such a revelation. Our search for God in the conversational reality of prayer is a mere answer we give to the gift of abundant and active love of God. It is true that the hermit seeks the Lord. In the course of time, however, he realizes more and more clearly a basic fact of the spiritual life: it is the Lord who seeks, even more intensely and originally, his poor human heart.

The presence of God, open to us as it is, is always prior to any human spiritual activity. It is always God who provokes the meeting with the human spirit. Our prayer would have been nonsense if its results had depended only on human efforts. What the hermit does first is to listen in faith to the speaking God, and then he ponders in his heart each of the words he has heard. The very act of listening to and pondering the words makes the meeting with the One we are seeking happen, because it is a meeting with the living voice of God. The word that is calling us not only reveals the face of the loved One. It is also a special place where God gives Himself to us in faith. So, we can say that for the hermit the whole process of seeking God is related to the profound practice of prayer, and it is a lesson in finding lost truth in the spirit of service.

5. The Necessity of Transformation

Undertaking the effort of walking the path of solitude, the hermit wants to meet the Lord truly and directly; he longs to see the Lord's face. It is because the hermit feels deeply, in the dimension of faith, that he is called to such a meeting. Only the gift of meeting the Person of Christ fully can soothe him and be a resting-place for him. In the deepest meaning of his calling, it turns out that it is God who is the essence of his freedom.

The epiphany of the face

Here, however, we encounter the problem of how it is possible to see God in this life. Is God accessible to our limited human perception? The Scripture says that nobody can see

God and live (cf. Ex 33:18-20; Jgs 13:22; Is 6:2).[13] For the hermit the meeting with the Creator entails giving up every single thing he has known, loved, aimed at, or taken as a foundation of his life so far. So, his meeting with the Creator means the death of his former existence and the taking on of a newly opened spiritual perspective. This experience of death, as we understand it here, is related to a certain change, an inner transformation or even a spiritual "revolution", which brands the hermit's future life – his search, his efforts, and his plans – with a lasting mark. His inner conversion is thus a profound purity of heart obtained as a gift and enabling him to perceive the One who is, in His very essence, the Imperceptible.

The search for God and the resulting renewal of heart lead us to the entrance of a mystery, where we attempt to perceive it with our whole self. This is a continuous effort to encounter a reality that infinitely eludes every endeavor to define or grasp it. This is an effort that takes place in the dark paths of theological faith and love. Faith should be described here firstly as an inner disposition to listen to the Word and secondly as faithfulness and a gift and sacrifice made of oneself. It is a submission to the secret activity of the Holy Spirit, who leads us for the meeting with unforeseen words and meanings. Such a submission requires a great personal maturity, wisdom, and humility, so that, having given up natural lights on our way to our aims, we can rely completely and exclusively on the action of the Spirit of love, truth, and goodness.

The whole severe life of the hermit, all his fasts, vigils, prayer, solitude, poverty, and silence, is to lead him to the face-to-face meeting with the secret presence of God. This

---

[13] Cf. ibid., pp. 69ff.

meeting is what the hermit is longing for and awaiting eagerly. But he realizes that there is only one place possible for such a meeting: the place that is a door through death to life, the place determined by the outstretched arms of the Cross.

That is why all the hermit's life efforts are hidden in the shadow of the Cross. Seeking for the living God and the final meeting and communion with Him means living in Christ, through whom and in whom we meet the Father. So meeting and seeing God are possible only through a gradual transformation of our being, which is brought about thanks to our participation in Christ's passion and in His death on the Cross. The hermit's Paschal experience includes thus the decision to give up his tenacious adherence to his own desires, hopes, or illusions. In other words, having been touched by the shadow of the Cross, we are able to leave our own selves and to go out, in complete openness and freedom, to meet the last things.

The touch of the Passover

If the hermit makes the decision for dying slowly, he does so because he believes with his whole heart in the Lord, who is the source of Life. The way of the desert, shadowed with the silhouette of the Cross, leads to the meeting with the risen Life, in which all the searching and toils of humanity find their ultimate aim, direction, and fullness. When the world of our egoism, illusions, and sin dies, we are able to read in a truly new light the words of St. Paul:

> For God, who said, "Light shall shine out of darkness," is the One who has shone in our hearts

> to give the light of the knowledge of the glory of
> God in the face of Christ.   (2 Cor 4:6)

One of the crucial moments of the hermit's journey consists in self-abandonment, motivated by the love of God and man. For the hermit, mortification and discipline are a helpful means to open wide his human heart to the reality of the truth and goodness. They also express the inner freedom and chastity of the person who now seeks not his own benefit, but the glory of the only Lord. Undoubtedly, living in solitude day by day has a trait of penance. But what it finally aims at above all is our inner conversion and transformation, which result in the human spirit's complete docility and subjection to the inspiration of the Divine truth. In any case penance cannot mean for the hermit an eccentric lifestyle, which would surprise or irritate others. His self-discipline ought never be a "gymnastic display", but rather the lesson of humility and wisdom of heart.

What the hermit desires most is to avoid disaster in his spiritual life: plunging into dreams and illusions. The down-to-earth character of the hermit's life should result from his constantly being in touch with things, which are both objective and very concrete in human existence. On the one hand, the vivid dynamism of the hermit's everyday life, which is the condition of its clarity and growth, feeds on its relation to the world of objective values. But on the other hand, the real meaning of the hermit's sacrifice and self-denial is based on the sober evaluation of his life conditions. That is why authentic Christian mortification always brings about a new quality of life.

The inner transformation that accompanies the hermit

on his journey consists in entrusting his human heart to God. That means a conscious and free participation in the process of ongoing life in the widest sense. So the complete response to the eremitic calling, with its character of free self-giving and sacrifice, is at the same time a profound inner protest against the degrading and lethal tumult of modern materialism. The path of eremitic discipline, besides all its other aims and meanings, is also to be a particular sign of protest, which awakens the world to the conscious and free existence deserving to be called human. All centuries – but especially our own times – have heard the voices of thoughtful people expressing their "no" against conventional and self-interested attitudes that characterize whole societies. That protest, which at first glance may seem to be fighting a losing battle, can, however, bear amazing fruit. In fact, it is a spiritual struggle for human freedom and universal solidarity, for the respect of the fundamental rights that guard human dignity.

The anchorite wants to awaken others to the authentic love that lies dormant at the bottom of every human heart. Love can be roused only by responding to the gift the person has received. So to rouse others to loving truly means to overcome the hegemony of power and money, the tyranny of greed and stupidity in human life. Love sets us free and opens our human spirit up to a free and conscious existence. In this way it enables us to actualize the social dimension of our lives. The love and wisdom that are born in the labor of the spiritual transformation give us a real opportunity to liberate human communities from the dictatorship of deceit and hatred. They open up a true perspective, setting us free from the necessity of a "herd life" of worshiping the gods of sexual pleasure, money, and technology.

The new optics

The Christian anchorite is not a gnostic, whose isolation from the world takes precedence in order that he can secure for himself the possibility of reaching "the land of pure spirituality". Such an approach is obviously an illusion which, detected too late, will certainly lead all who adopt it to spiritual disaster. Even provided that we agree on the illusionary character of the created world, such an assumption may be justified only if we take into account its relativity. It is true that created things can deceive and beguile us, though it is not because they are deceitful all by themselves, but because the human heart, tangled up in webs of sin and greed, is eager to take pleasure and satisfaction in them. The anchorite never gives up and renounces the world of things out of contempt for them. He does so in order to achieve the inner space necessary to appreciate their real value and inner beauty.

Leaving the world and inner renunciation are the path to discovering the logic and the truth of the created world. Fathoming inner structures and meanings, the hermit realizes still more clearly that the ultimate value of the world is not constituted by the world itself, but it transcends the world boundlessly. What is essential for a human being is the perception of things that last and are eternal. What is needed is a certain distance providing space for an authentic freedom of mind and heart, in order to perceive the world and all its problems in truth and love, which means in God. By finding the whole creation at its very Source, the hermit becomes a person able to contemplate. The hermit's contemplation of reality is his special way of perceiving it through the eyes of faith. This kind of perception reveals to him the rays of

God's magnificence and glory. The contemplative approach towards the truth about one's self and the truth about others actualizes the Gospel's message about God's kingdom, which is already present in the world. This truth, however, should be understood and proclaimed not just verbally or intellectually, but above all by means of humbly accepting the gift of our own existence. The acceptance of the gift brings about the inner necessity of giving it back to its donor in love. The need to make such a sacrifice is the essence of Christian ascetic life and inner conversion.

Seeking God in the way of the eremitic life is, in a sense, a constant struggle against the demon of despair, a struggle that is possible only through personal conversion. We are able to overcome despair only thanks to the power that radiates from the Cross and thanks to the hope that comes with it. Inasmuch as we acknowledge that the despair of sinful human existence is in fact a bottomless abyss, we must go out into the desert ready to make constant sacrifice and taking an attitude of humble trust. Sacrifice and trust are founded on Christ and on His victory, which brings in abundance the rays of true joy for the modern world. Joy has its source in an inner transformation and in experiencing the spirit of Christ's blessings, and what it brings is an authentic spiritual detachment and freedom.

The hermit is a person fascinated with the Lord's beauty, which becomes perceivable and clear only for a heart transformed by the power of grace. So the call to constant conversion becomes the hermit's necessity, one of the most essential needs he discovers in himself. Eventually, the hermit's sincere acceptance of Christ's proposal calling for inner transformation and conversion turns out to be the surest way of proclaiming the Kingdom. "The time is fulfilled, and the kingdom of God is at hand; repent and believe in the gospel." (Mk 1:15) The words are addressed firstly to those who do not know Christ yet, but the anchorite takes them as an actual call addressed to him. He understands well the necessity of constant purification; making an effort towards his still deeper conversion, the hermit becomes a clear sign of God's glory present in the world.

Jesus' call to penance and conversion, as it was with the calling of the Prophets, does not refer mainly to concrete outer deeds, ascetic practices, or "sackcloth and ashes". Rather, the calling in its essence refers firstly to a serious need for spiritual change, and so it reveals the inner dimension of penance. All outer ascetic practices, whether signs, gestures, or penitential deeds, can only result from it. For the hermit inner conversion means a grace-motivated effort towards changing his entire existence; it means a radical return to God by giving up the sin that his conscience is charged with. This change is often accompanied by a salutary pain and sorrow, which the Fathers of the Church called sorrow of the soul (*animi cruciatus*) and contrition of the heart (*compunctio cordis*).

III

FOUNDATIONS OF THE EREMITIC EXPERIENCE

Going out into the desert and withdrawing from the conventional course of affairs makes sense only when it leads to the still fuller experience and love of the Trinity. The hermit tries to be as close to the Holy Trinity as possible; his life, love, and finally his death are a kind of beautiful testimony given to the Father through the Son in the Holy Spirit. The hermit's life, immersed in the reality of the Triune God, reflects in a basic way the message and the incarnation of the Word.

1. The Desire for Salvation

Therefore, the eremitic experience is, to a certain extent, marked by the Passover, which means salvation. The desert indicates a decision to leave everything that is banal, hollow, and sinful in human existence. In other words, the horizon of the desert is the line separating all that is not redeemed from the realm of eternal meanings, which is the realm of salvation. The mystery of Christ's Passover, the mystery of His life, death, and resurrection, becomes, step by step, present in the hermit's life. In this way it takes the form of a meaningful testimony to the evangelical truth. A testimony of this kind has its source in an elementary desire of the human heart: the desire for salvation.

Spiritual therapy

The overwhelming desire for salvation never results from our human, merely natural resourcefulness. Such a desire can only be born in people who feel deeply how insufficient and slight they are in their human existence. Human existence, fragile and limited as it is by nature, needs to be completed and strengthened by something limitless and eternal. The burning desire for salvation can arise only in those who search sincerely the paths of faith, so it is in those who are already under the influence of God's Spirit.

In fact there is much to say about the Christian hermit – who he is, what his basic motives are, what his day is like, what the meaning of prayer is in his life. But all that is incomplete unless we relate it to the hermit's elementary and profound need to reach the fullness of his faith, which is salvation. The hermit encounters his poverty and frailty, and so he desires to be healed. Before he sets off on his journey, before he undertakes his difficult spiritual challenge, he needs to be healed of the wounds inflicted by sin. So, the fervent desire for our own conversion and salvation is the first condition of going out into the desert.

Opening himself up by faith to the Holy Spirit, the hermit finds a kind of two-layered structure to his own existence. His existence is stretched out between the layer of his everyday human life and the layer which is unreachable directly but which is his ultimate target: God. To experience such an existential condition means to encounter the mystery of our own life and to realize that we are not able to fathom it unaided. Facing the mystery of our existence, we face the question that we constitute for ourselves. This is the question we need to answer affirmatively.

The eremitic life, in which the elementary factors of human existence are highlighted so strongly, is undoubtedly an excellent tool to provide "a key" to that riddle. One never knows how long it will take for the hermit to find "the key" and to realize that the riddle of his own being cannot be solved except in relation to community. In any case, our affirmative answer to the question of life's mystery is possible only when given in the perspective of salvation, in the full sense of the word. Here such a perspective is constituted by our complete spiritual openness to the grace of redemption.

When the hermit awakens in himself the ardent desire for salvation, he sets off at the same time to meet the riddle of his own being. He gets a chance to find eternal fulfillment in his life in relation to the mystery of the Holy Trinity. What always precedes the desire for salvation is touching God in faith. We can never long for anybody or anything that lies beyond the limits of our experience. So to be able to accept salvation means to be able to have a faith that opens us up to the reality of God's mystery. It is also a positive attitude adopted through our personal freedom, an attitude of saying "yes" to the grace of redemption.

Eventually, the hermit sets off to meet the very foundation of human freedom: to meet God. No matter how vague and dark God's presence may seem to us, we know that He is here directly for us. The eremitic experience, motivated by the original desire for salvation, should as it were naturally take the form of prayer and contemplation. Prayer, which is a meeting and a dialogue with God, is the space where we become more truly ourselves and so come closer to salvation. As we accept the grace that opens us to the realm of the Trinity, we find ourselves in a situation of salvation. From that moment on, we live "before" and "for" the absolute community of the Persons.[14]

The drama of existence

To describe the eremitic experience in this perspective, we can use some useful terms taken from our everyday relationships with others. These are presence, meeting, and dialogue. Christian salvation takes place on the plane of mutual presence and meeting between God and man. So searching for salvation in the way of the desert inevitably has the form of a drama, where two freedoms – divine and human – interact with each other in a whole range of different relationships and attitudes. In fact, the hermit becomes an actor in the *Theodrama*, which still unfolds in the Trinitarian mystery. The *Theodrama* is a process of exchanging love, which goes on eternally in the bosom of the Holy Trinity. So God's turning towards man, the dynamism of the saving care that the Creator has for the world, becomes a drama that involves human existence. The hermit's only chance to work out his salvation is to engage in God's human drama wholeheartedly.

Therefore, what constitutes the eremitic life is searching

---

[14] Cf. Tomasz Węcławski, *Obecność i spotkanie* (Poznań, 1981), pp. 50, 60.

for the absolute Presence, which becomes the environment of our salvation. To enjoy the possibility of meeting fully the redeeming God is to enjoy the possibility of love. So, the realm of love gives us a chance to interact with others in full openness, concern, and dialogue. Only in this way can we eventually come to the point of entrusting ourselves to the other person and accepting the other person's gift of self. Mutual understanding and acceptance depend on the depth and intensity of the relationship. The silent presence of the persons who have mutually entrusted themselves to each other gives birth to community and devotion. Thus what the hermit waits for in the desert is the saving Presence that gives Itself as a gift. Love is an enlivening power, and the hermit accepts it willingly. But what is special about love is its Paschal character, which deprives us of our own being and gives us the gift of a new life. This means that it raises us from the dead. Here we can see more clearly the process of gradually forsaking ourselves, the process of leaving all that is wasteful, unfruitful, and ill-disposed in order to find the original dynamism of life.

Eventually, seeking salvation in the way of the eremitic life is related directly to seeking God, savior of the world and its people. The hermit discovers gradually, through his everyday experience, that a state of grace and salvation means accepting in ourselves God's energy of unifying love. One who gains salvation is a person whose entire existence has been encompassed by the dynamism of Trinitarian life. The one who loves sees his own reflection in the loved one. Saving love does not annihilate those embraced by it and does not erase the unique richness of their subjective beauty. The essence of love consists rather in the mutual permeation of two freedoms: the divine and the human. They are both, so to speak, transparent to each other, and therefore they make possible a mutual "life-in-self".

In seeking God, the hermit consciously enters a drama. Only in this way is the deep relationship of entrusting and accepting made possible. A personal relationship of love based on the mutual openness of the two freedoms is an unfathomable mystery. As Kierkegaard wrote:

> Just as God dwells in a light from which flows every ray that illuminates the world, yet no one can force his way along these paths in order to see God, since the paths of light turn into darkness when one turns toward the light – so love dwells in hiding or is hidden in the innermost being. Just so the gush of the spring lures by the murmuring persuasion of its rippling, indeed almost pleads with a person to walk along that path and not inquisitively want to force his way in to find its source and disclose its secret. [15]

There is something childlike in the hermit that makes him feel dependent on God in every single aspect of his life. The hermit wants to live in simplicity and truth, and that means firstly to confess before God his own weakness and limitation, which cannot be overcome by human means. The hermit is a sinner who longs for salvation, who feels confused and helpless in seeking the lost God. Seeing oneself in the truth and sincere acceptance of one's fragility is the most

---

[15] S. Kierkegaard, "Love's Hidden Life and Its Recognizability by Its Fruits," in *Kierkegaard's Writings* (Princeton, New Jersey, 1995), vol. XVI titled *Works of Love*, First Series, chapter I, p. 9.

important condition of receiving the grace of salvation. The human helplessness that is revealed in meeting God turns out to be the way of possibly receiving the grace of redemption. In fact, there is only one way of salvation: the way of Christ. Experiencing the helplessness of our own existence is the way of the Cross that, if fully accepted, leads us to salvation. For the hermit the way of the Cross is usually connected with situations where we are set free from all the illusions we fostered for so many years of our life. The Cross means the necessity of leaving the "paper world", which we built so eagerly and which is now collapsing like a house of cards. The Cross eventually means our courage to acknowledge the failure of all our efforts to construct our life according only to our own ideas and fantasies.

The gift of salvation that God offers us is the fruit of God's absolute love for people and for the world. So, it is never any kind of prize for "being good". The logic of saving love exceeds all the limits of human comprehension and evaluation. In the light of this logic it turns out that the sun shines more brightly where the darkness is blacker, grace abounds even more where sin increases, and salvation is given to those who feel they are completely unworthy of it. Only the broken vessel of the human heart can become a place of revelation of love's enlivening power. What is needed is the moment when we realize that God is the only one who can give us salvation and change our very weakness into an amazingly fertile soil. By accepting the grace of salvation we learn to be humble, through humility we attain understanding, and finally wisdom brings God's power of compassion and love into our hearts.

By accepting the grace of salvation, the hermit accepts God's motherly tenderness, delicacy, and love, and starts extending them to the people he meets. As a result, he cares sincerely for others' good and has compassion for their weaknesses and sins. Having himself experienced salvation, the hermit wants to share it delicately and humbly with other people.

It is in fact difficult to say what this merciful love really is that starts to determine the hermit's life. It is much easier to experience it than to define it. In any case, in the hermit's life merciful love takes the form of patience and delicacy. So nobody is condemned, but everybody is accepted and strengthened. The loving heart is the heart that cares for other people's good and is ready to serve for the salvation of the world. The ocean of human needs far exceeds the reach of one humble anchorite's readiness to serve. But this ocean has been embraced by the saving might of Christ, who is the very source of mercy and the source of every gift. As a gift, mercy still has to be granted and accepted in the experience of faith. So its dynamism calls for continuous acknowledgment and engagement and cannot be brought down to the level of objects. As von Hildebrand writes:

> It is devoting my heart and giving my own life – in the sense that the beloved person becomes the center of my life and a source of the most particular happiness, so that my happiness becomes dependent on the other. The highest form of such devotion can be found in God's love for men. It is also characteristic of spousal love. Then it can be encountered anywhere – in any deep and intense kind of natural love. The

devotion is simply a trait of love, since the beloved person, whoever she or he may be, becomes the center of my life. [16]

2. The Moment of Self-Denial

We enter solitude searching for mercy, tenderness, and simplicity, but when all is said and done, to find salvation. There is no space for any diplomacy or pretence here. Liberating himself from any routine, from schemes and habits, the hermit attempts to enter a new reality and wants to step into a new dimension of space and time. His heart opens towards eternal things. The desert makes it possible to leave behind the profane world and, at the same time, to open up onto the horizon of a new order, the horizon of reality that is incomprehensible and untouchable. The perspective of God's absolute glory, which unfolds before the hermit's eyes, gives him a foretaste of eternity. Despite his existence being firmly fixed in the specific matters of time and everyday life, the hermit touches simultaneously – not to say above all – the eternal aspect of human existence.

The necessity of asceticism

Of course finding the ultimate perspective of the human condition, which means finding God hidden in the depths of the human heart, is never without our actual ascetic efforts. In fact, the eremitic way is always related to following in the footsteps of Christ. The hermit walks along his Lord's path, which leads him up a mountain peak. This is the mountain

---

[16] D. von Hildebrand, *Das Wesen der Liebe*, p. 486; quoted after T. Gadacz, loc.cit.,p.36.

of both humiliation and glorification. This is the path of poverty, obedience, and humility that goes to the point of the scandal of the Cross. The inner simplicity and poverty of the hermit manifests itself in his ardent desire to be stripped of everything, including his own "self", just for the love of Christ.

What is necessary at the beginning is to set ourselves free from our everyday routine and our lifestyle, which we have adhered to for so many years. However, while going out to the desert to attain our inner freedom, we need to be careful of easily adopting some new "eremitic" routines and conventions in our behavior and reactions. They could become another form of spiritual blockage and passivity. In fact, the eremitic life should be based on strict order and a daily schedule. The anchorite needs to have specific times designated for prayer, meals, work, and rest. But the strict order should serve the hermit's spiritual purposes and not be an impediment to the spiritual life. What is necessary here is a good grasp of priorities. The hermit cannot accept a situation where he becomes a servant to his own guidelines, projects, or ideas, as "saintly" as they may be. What his spiritual progress is measured by is his spontaneous readiness to abandon all his chores immediately when somebody knocks at his hermitage door. The one who knocks at the door is always the Lord present in our neighbor.

By his openness to God and God's works, the hermit wants to be fully accessible to everybody. Such an attitude springs from the gift of constant prayer, which enlivens his humble heart. Enjoying undisturbed dialogue with the Lord and sanctifying each of his ordinary days with prayer, the hermit becomes God's signpost for the world, because his life radiates the light of Christ. The anchorite participates in the freedom of God, in the freedom that comes from abandoning one's own will and entrusting oneself completely to God. Thanks to his inner simplicity and his freedom from any attachment, the hermit is able to look out with new eyes and see the Lord's features in the face of every other person.

The hermit's freedom makes him innocent and at the same time defenseless. Such defenselessness is directly related to his simplicity and freedom. As a matter of fact, it is impossible to hurt such a person, because his humility makes him a perfect example of mercy and forgiveness. His face is always bright, calm, and fresh, and he never loses heart or buoyancy of spirit. That strength of his does not spring from any particular mystical aptitude. It is deeply rooted in the peace and rest he experiences, and his peace and rest is the Lord Himself.

Everything that has been said so far about life in solitude turns our attention to the character of *kenosis* that this kind of life bears. That leads us to the special importance of self-abandonment and inner poverty. The very fact of going out into the desert is a clear expression of the inner desire and effort to attain full spiritual freedom that is accessible only in Christ. The desert, whatever it may consist of, however its specific colors may be painted, whatever may influence its inner dynamism – all of that is a constant memento of *kenosis*. The self-abandonment and inner smallness the hermit enters into just for the sake of love are intended to introduce him into an attitude that the Church traditionally calls holy indifference and peace of heart. In fact the hermit can never possess peace of heart and the freedom that comes with it once and for all. They are the task he must undertake again and again for all his life.

Inner smallness

The spiritual poverty that is an aspect of *kenosis* consists in the effort to renounce one's desires, hopes, plans, and needs. It is an attitude of total self-abandonment and detachment, with a view to getting ready to do God's will.[17] In a sense it is the attitude of spiritual dying that finally bears the fruit of the fullness of life in Christ. It is not only that the hermit day by day faces death, but also that he consciously chooses this process of dying that goes ever deeper and deeper as an element of his everyday life. At the moment when the flame of God's presence is kindled before our eyes, we become aware of how transient and insignificant all our plans and hopes are if they are made without the consideration of God's will and love. At this moment, deep in our hearts we develop the desire for *kenosis*, an inner smallness that we can positively describe as a peaceful and trustful consent to God's work both in our individual lives and in the world.

Our human *kenosis* springs from our hope of resurrection; so to experience poverty and the inner lowliness as a gift of grace is to tear off the veils of fear. When the hermit opens his heart to the fullness of God's Word, he overcomes his fear because, through the grace of the Word, he can accept any possible aspect of God's will towards him. So his consent must include acceptance of the possibility of death as a sign and testimony given to truth and love.

This openness of heart is possible, of course, only for somebody who has spent most of his life searching for the

---

[17] Cf. Catherine De Hueck Doherty, *Poustinia: Christian Spirituality of the East for Western Man* (Ave Maria Press, 1975); quoted after C. De Hueck Doherty, *Pustynia* (Warsaw, 1991), pp. 109ff.

Lord. It can be experienced by the mature traveler who has overcome all the ambushes, temptations, and wrong turns that he has encountered, more or less consciously, on his way. The desert, simple and harsh as it is, educates a person in freedom, which manifests itself by the fact that we are not attached any more to other people's opinions and judgments. The hermit has to stay immune to the great idol called public opinion. Praised or humiliated, raised up or pushed down, he is constantly at peace, and he does not let his heart be disturbed in its meekness and concentration.

Kerygma

When one is not attached to fears or the opinions of others, the fruit of his spiritual joy and freedom can grow. The inner space and silence open the ears of his heart and enable him to start listening. And it is then when the one who is engrossed in the meaning of the Word becomes ready and eager to proclaim the good news, the Gospel of Jesus Christ, the life and the truth. The anchorite, led by God's Holy Spirit, receives the power to proclaim the Word of God. He realizes that *kerygma* is one of the most difficult aspects of his inner lowliness. Spiritually mature as he is, the anchorite believes that it is the Lord who is going to speak and who is going to proclaim the Kingdom through His servant's lips. The human word is in service of the Word of God; all that is small and weak is suddenly raised up to the fullness of God's glory and thus gains God's power and effectiveness. Here we can sense in a way the mystery of this special and amazing power of the hermit's words and actions. They are so powerful despite their simplicity, kindness, and apparent awkwardness. If only they spring from inner lowliness and humility, they have prophetic power. The hermit renounces his own human word and in silence and solitude he turns moment by moment into fertile soil, ready to receive the seed of God's Word. At that moment when he feels he is called to speak out, his words always refer to the eternal things: truth and beauty.

What the hermit says comes from the depths of his heart and it contains the words given him by God. This does not mean, however, that they are either solemn or exceptional words. Usually the words are simple and delicate and have nothing to do with the proud speeches of the wise men of this world. The charism of the desert consists in the gift of understanding and discerning an interlocutor's spiritual needs. What the hermit says is rooted in the fact that he wants to help the other person in need. There are times when his words are full of compassion, mild and supportive, and there are other moments when they have to be strict and harsh. But whatever he says, he knows that his words express a gift of wisdom received from his Lord.

Affirmation

Inner smallness, *kenosis*, does not bear the fruit of spiritual emptiness, which would have led the hermit astray and pushed him into deep neurosis. The visible fruit of *kenosis* is a growing peace and an inner energy that enable the hermit to undertake ever-new tasks. A pure heart, which the hermit receives as the result of giving his own will and mind up to God, surely manifests itself in his holy indifference and his freedom from all the matters of this world. The pure heart, however, does not deprive him of initiative and energy when action is necessary. But what is crucial and characteristic in the different tasks he undertakes is that he does not really care about the fruit of his actions. He is not attached to and he is, in a way, spiritually indifferent to their future results. The way of self-abandonment, which the hermit enters and which is one of the main paths of his everyday struggle, does not consist simply in negation and bringing reality down to a state of non-existence. Even if some spiritual paths seem to direct him to such a point, they are surely not the paths of a disciple of Christ. It is not negating or disregarding the created reality that determines the goal of the Christian spiritual way. The reality is always a gift from our Creator. The Christian goal consists in offering up everything to God in complete freedom and love. That can be practiced by keeping a proper distance from the world and all worldly matters. Our freedom has a particular meaning here. It is not a free choice of this or that possibility, but it means being totally at God's disposal and in dialogue with Him. Such freedom connotes a complete openness toward the absolute freedom of God Himself.

Thanks to openness, which essentially depends on our faith's maturity, we can progress step by step in the difficult art of deciphering Divine Providence's plans for us and for the whole world. The inner sensibility and simplicity of the hermit, his mind and his will, gradually turn toward the Word that eventually becomes for him the only acceptable reference point and signpost. A radical and clear-cut decision to listen to the Word and to ignore all other voices, including the whispering voice of our own "self", is the first decisive step we take on the path to follow Christ authentically. Kenotic smallness calls for human freedom in order to engage it directly and constantly on behalf of absolute freedom. We have Christ as the perfect example of giving up His freedom to the Father.

In any case, the process of deep purification and the freedom connected with it are the fruits of God's hidden action in us. And what God quite often uses here is our experience of different temptations. That is why the purification that leads to freedom requires us to be persistent and brave in our spiritual struggle against ourselves and against the devil. This struggle has several stages, in which we are not always victorious. The hermit then goes through many critical points, and each crisis is what determines his consequent route: whether he is going to continue in the way of the desert or to quit it completely.

As the hermit's faith and love develop, he discovers the ultimate goal of *kenosis*. Namely, what he learns is that the whole smallness he has accepted is closely related to his ardent desire to experience the Passion of Christ. The only thing the mature hermit longs for is to follow his Master on the Way of the Cross.

So here is still another instance in which we see that psychological, sociological, or cultural terms are far too limited for explaining the essence of the eremitic calling. Its full meaning and exceptionality can be revealed only from the perspective of Christ's Paschal Mystery. The hermit follows the path of faith, and this is where he hopes to meet God and salvation. Searching for ultimate meaning and fulfillment, he opens himself up to the chance of personal change offered to him in faith. The dynamism of inner growth, based on giving up all that is limited for the sake of greater things and all objects for the sake of personal values, is structured according to Christ's Passion. The eremitic way is most of all a testimony to both inner smallness and the light of God's revealing glory. So it stays in close relation to the realm of the Passion seen as progressing from a life of slavery and sin to the fullness of the gift of salvation.

3. The Truth as the Way of Humility

We venture the opinion that the interest the people of our time take in the eremitic experience illustrates a kind of spiritual longing for a world not directly altered by technology and rationalism. This is as it were a spiritual thirst for discovering the realm called mystery. We are positive that Christian eremitism properly understood gives us, through its mature practice of faith and love, the possibility of "touching" still closer God's mystery. This mystery is the reality of the Truth and Freedom that are demonstrated by the Christian faith. Undoubtedly, hermits are people who aim at subjecting their whole lives to the definite requirements of God's Truth.

The reality of truth

The eremitic life seen in such a way must be free from any schemes and conventions and must introduce us to the space of creativity. It makes possible the finding of the seeds of truth and freedom scattered in the world. By learning how to be humble, which he achieves by bending his steps toward the truth about himself and the world, the hermit does not look for the sublime ideas of some philosophical systems. For him the truth is rather a matter of a personal relationship. Christian humility is born when we bring ourselves closer and closer to the Truth that is essentially a Communion of Persons, and that enlivens the whole created world and determines the ultimate meaning of human existence. For the hermit, the light of truth is the light of God's Revelation.

We can say that modern civilization is struggling with an elusive, but at the same time quite concrete, ghost of despondency and faithlessness. When we cast doubt on the very possibility of our creative upbuilding of the world in truth and love, we arouse fear and a sense of insecurity. On the one hand, modern people appreciate new qualities of life and would like to practice a new lifestyle based on simplicity and truth. On the other hand, they have doubts about realizing such a possibility and may not believe that a life of freedom, justice, and truth can really come true. This is a paranoid state of spiritual slavery, which can lead straight to despair. As we see it, the eremitic experience means a constant effort to overcome the abyss of despair, which yawns somewhere there at the bottom of the human heart. To overcome it is to light up the horizon of our existence by the power of the Christian humility and trust that spring from Christ's Passion.

The struggle that the hermit carries on against the demon of despair turns out to be a struggle against what he has called so far "his very self". Where the shadow of despair is cast from is the very center of human existence wounded by pride. We can confront our fears and despair only if we strongly believe that it is really possible to extirpate the sin of deception from our human lives, the sin of deception called pride. Struggling against despair, the hermit struggles against himself. He tries to overcome the darkness of untruthfulness that impedes his liveliness and energy. He wants to come out of the dusk of falsity and begin a new life. He does not want to hide any more from God, from the world, and from himself, and he yearns to light up all the spheres of his fragile existence with the light of truth.

Humility

Human pride is the result of a lack of understanding of ourselves, the result of an approach that views reality in a distorted perspective, one based on our greedy "ego". We therefore need to be healed and changed, we need a new perspective, a new way of perceiving and evaluating. We need this change to enable us to base reality not on "I" and our own personal needs, but on God, the original source of the truth. And this is the humility the Christian hermit aims at. But what path can lead us to this priceless and incomparable virtue?

Humility for the hermit, like anything of value, is a gift received in faith. In the light of revealed truth, what eventually gives us a new perception is the grace of faith. The hermit gets to know himself under the rays of Christ's truth and acknowledges his own poverty and a kind of deep inner powerlessness on two levels: the existential and the moral. The hermit sees his helplessness, but he does not run from it. Rather he entrusts it to God and asks the Lord to change it in his own mysterious way. For the hermit humility is a faith-motivated decision to base his whole dynamic life on a brave search for the meaning of life in the broadest existential sense, to be found uniquely in God – to the exclusion of everything that comes from the created world.

Being a grace, humility can be born in us when we truly meet God in faith. We can discover the truth in the light of God's Word, but only if we acknowledge our human powerlessness and the fragility of our life. In fact, the truth goes much deeper and reveals our identity much more fully. By the grace of meeting the mystery of the One and Triune God, the hermit can understand the meaning and the unique value of "God's own image", which is the most crucial aspect of the personal "I". So humility, above all else, gives us access to the most intimate corners of our existence, which the Book of Revelation describes as getting "a new name". The "new name" expresses the essence of our Christian calling and God's gracious choice.

The virtue of humility is what enables the hermit to keep a safe distance from the humdrum and the everyday preoccupations of the world. Being able to see the deeper meaning of ongoing problems allows the hermit to be at peace when faced with the many different pressures that each day brings. This is an ability to evaluate things properly and to relate them all to the supreme value: to the Truth. So humility is that attitude of the human spirit that enables the hermit to find his identity – to be himself. "Be yourself" for the hermit is not just another overused slogan, made meaningless by the world of business. "Be yourself" is an attitude that springs from a pure heart that enables us to rejoice in the luminous glory of Christ's face. "Be yourself" is the ability to decipher our true identity as it relates to God and to the world.

It is when we meet God's love that we are awakened and called to be humble. It is then that we can set off on our search for the truth, but only when we have been touched by God's love. Humility is also one of the most definitive virtues of Christian perfection, one that crowns the way of the desert. Quite possibly the virtue of humility will be not only the condition of a fruitful realization of the hermit's calling, but also the condition of a fruitful and fuller realization of God's kingdom on earth. The possibility of implementing the Good News in the world is linked directly to our readiness to accept Christ's truth, a truth so difficult but at the same time so simple and obvious, a truth that sets us free.

Humility comes with an understanding of the truth about God, the world, and ourselves. When we know the truth, it sets us free (Jn 8:32). Humility is the path on which the hermit can learn how to be skilled in following the trail of freedom. The desert, wild as it is, with its endless sands, naked rocks, raging storms, and its limitless horizon gives a true sense of freedom. Who knows this mysterious sense of freedom better than a nomad tired of wandering? But the hermit reaches for another kind of freedom, a freedom that is not limited by time or space, because it is a freedom of the Spirit.

Towards freedom

Undoubtedly, the history of human thought beginning with German idealism has been marked by many who have made an effort to determine the scope and essence of freedom. Philosophers, sociologists, psychologists, theologians, and cultural theorists continue to try to present us with many different interpretations of that reality called freedom. But it seems that in the process of chasing after freedom, freedom itself is lost. Somebody once said that in fact people run away from freedom. Indeed, is not going away to a hermitage and closing the door of a barren cell a kind of escape from all the responsibilities, decisions, and choices of life, ones often having momentous consequences? Is there not a hint here of alienation and escape, a sign of neurosis perhaps?

Here we have to stress that in a hermit's life freedom takes the form of a Person: the Holy Spirit. So for the hermit, freedom is rooted in a personal relationship with God, as well as with other people. That is why freedom is something so much greater than just a mere possibility to choose. Of course the immense potential of the freedom that we have received, simply as a gift, is realized through concrete choices, though our human freedom goes far beyond the mere choices we make.

The freedom of the desert implies that we are open and ready to receive God, the ultimate meaning of our existence, and the one and only way to fulfill our life completely. So, for the hermit freedom is a kind of loving openness, which acknowledges and consciously accepts that there exists a truth far greater than oneself. The Christian hermit does not look for freedom in silence, solitude, and fasting, neither does he look for it in himself or in other people. It is possible, of course, to find sparks of truth at the bottom of one's own heart, in our relations with others, or in the physical world. However, these are only little rays of sunlight that shine afar off, somewhere on the horizon of things and events. So when we touch freedom, we touch the mystery that is God, and thus we can be free as long as we accept eternal things, which depends on our faith. The hermit does not just experience freedom inside himself but in the Holy Spirit, who is the Giver of life and love. Having experienced the freedom of love, we realize that all other kinds of freedom are rooted in it and draw their lifeblood from it. Freedom is an untarnished heart's ability to accept Revelation.

The experience of being liberated by Christ's truth

leads us to a desire to do the will of God. Thus it becomes clear that sin means rejecting the freedom given to us by the Holy Spirit. Therefore the eremitic life is a realization of the full spiritual freedom that expresses itself in joy, a kind of lightheartedness, a peace with no attachments. By choosing solitude and silence, the hermit in fact stands up for a freedom that is God. It is not possible to find authentic freedom in the everyday business of life, on a superficial plane, with one's ears full of the everyday. The modern world offers an endless number of temptations that separate us from freedom. Freedom is born in the solitude and silence that is God. The desert makes for such an existential perspective, which provides a favorable environment in which to mature to an authentic freedom. So the desert is not just a safe haven or a hiding place, but a liberating space. The desert cannot therefore be taken as a synonym for getting lost, isolated or neurotic. The desert horizon is wide enough to encompass all those spheres of our human spirit that open us to the approaching Mystery – Freedom.

4. Returning to Paradise

In the Christian tradition the act of going into the desert, into solitude and silence, has been compared to searching for Paradise lost. In their theological teachings the Church Fathers – St. Irenaeus, Origen, and St. Ambrose – often illustrate the hermit's experience by the image of one returning to Paradise.[18] We should remember, however, that such a symbolic view was but one step in the search and not the final fulfillment; for the Fathers, the return to Paradise

---

[18] Cf. L. Bouyer, op. cit., p. 47.

was only a transitional stage on the road to the fullness of salvation. This image illustrates the human longing for the restoration of inner justice and holiness.

Original justice

The Book of Genesis raises the question as to whether in our present life we can attain such a level of inner purity that would make it possible for us to be with God just as Adam was in Paradise. Having committed that first sin, can we ever reach such a level of spiritual maturity that our faith would enable us to feel God's presence at every single moment of our life? Is a return to Paradise possible? According to the Fathers of the Church the answer is "yes". The great exodus to the desert that happened at the turn of the 4th century was essentially evidence of people convinced that a return to original innocence and sanctity was possible. They strove for a communion with God such as would be a reflection of Paradise, a unity only possible thanks to Christ's grace.

The starting point on the road back to original innocence was conversion, a change of heart. In order to enter the way of Christ, the way of the Gospel, people had to give up their sins; only then could they attain full communion with God. In the hermit's heart the return to Paradise bore a most delicious spiritual fruit: wisdom. Since hermits have always been regarded as wise men, people have always turned to them for advice in times of need. In Egypt there were disciples thirsty for "the word" of their Abba; in Russia questions about the ways of prayer were addressed to startsy, and intellectuals came to these elders in search of the hope they had lost. Today, in our

Godless world, the hermit can be a light that shows the way, that guides us beyond a "McDonald's civilization".

The spirit of wisdom

The hermit follows wisdom, for it makes his faith prove true and enables him to practice in real life the truth that he preaches. That is why the hermit's everyday life must be a clear and legible picture of the truth he affirms and trusts. Only such a life makes a hermit trustworthy in the eyes of other people, who will not always share his beliefs and values. What can attract them and what wins their trust is the power of faith. The hermit, living in harmony with God and himself, understands more fully and completely the ways of life and of the world. In other words, no human experience is foreign to him. Surely we remember different prophets, hermits, and sages known from fairy tales and legends, figures utterly remote from our time. The modern world has discarded them, considering them moth-eaten characters, unmissed and unwanted. Instead, it has created thousands of new gurus, who are trusted and followed blindly. The scientist's wary eye and the intellectual's critical mind can earn our trust, but they can sometimes also scare us.

A growing interest by some in Oriental methods of meditation and an explosion of new charismatic movements in the Church make us think, however, that there is still somewhere, at the bottom of the human heart, a dormant desire for true wisdom. But we cannot find wisdom overnight: we have to mature. St. Paul, while delving into his heart and pondering on the mysterious reality of wisdom, says:

> Yet we do speak wisdom among those who are

> mature; a wisdom, however, not of this age, nor
> of the rulers of this age, who are passing away; but
> we speak God's wisdom in a mystery, the hidden
> wisdom, which God predestined before the ages
> to our glory; the wisdom which none of the
> rulers of this age has understood; for if they had
> understood it, they would not have crucified the
> Lord of glory. (1 Cor 2:6-9)

The eremitic life, viewed as a charism of the Holy Spirit, gives us the possibility of experiencing the wisdom that St. Paul described. Wisdom is never the fruit of human effort and diligence but a gift, a supernatural understanding that comes with contemplation. Therefore wisdom is the result of a simple perception of reality, intuitive, vague and amorphous, but at the same time animated by a mature love. It comes as the fruit of a prayerful communion with God and brings complete peace and fulfillment. It is a kind of loving understanding that, as a gift, becomes the silent indication of a spiritual beauty that we can trace only in the solitude and silence of the desert.

Christian wisdom, born out of the eremitic experience, enables us to take a fresh look at the state of the world: a look, however, that is not limited to watching the world passively but rather involves entrusting the world completely into the tender hands of the Providence of the Father. This experience of wisdom becomes a kind of abandonment resulting from a new understanding of life in all its detail. Firstly, that means giving up our own plans, passions, and habit of trying to rationalize everything in our lives. And secondly, it means understanding that we have to accept the gift of salvation for ourselves and for the whole world, because we are unable to go forward without it. Christian wisdom is regarded by many in the world as foolishness. It is the attitude of a child completely dependent on the God with a motherly face, the God who carefully embraces a little baby in His gentle arms (Is 49:15). This is a foretaste of the joy of Paradise, and yet it is not the end of the hermit's journey.

We can experience such wisdom in contemplation that springs from living faith and love. On the one hand, a strong faith protects us against a gnostic temptation to lock mysteries within concepts. On the other hand, faith is the only effective "tool" to open hearts to the light of wisdom and to acceptance of the gift of spiritual understanding. The moment when we consciously let God take the initiative in our lives, we have a sure sign that wisdom is in our hearts. Our efforts then should concentrate on clearing the way for that process to begin.

The gift of wisdom brings the hermit so close to the loving Father that His divine presence becomes concrete and touchable, and the anchorite is able to enter on a new path that leads to communion with God. This contemplative meeting requires an inner concentration where all obstacles – words, concepts, or images – are eradicated. It is a trusting immersion of oneself in an absolute silence that is a simple and free state of being. The hermit does not enter into an existential emptiness, a complete passivity, or a state of annihilation. His silence is a loving, persevering presence, a peaceful attention and patient waiting for the coming of Christ. The wisdom of Christian life means to meet "the flame of love", a love that introduces a person into a space of silence and solitude. St. John of the Cross explains the essence of that experience in the following way:

This flame of love is the Spirit of its Bridegroom, who is the Holy Spirit. The soul feels Him within itself not only as a fire that has consumed and transformed it but as a fire that burns and flares within it.[19]

5. Love Overcomes Death

Longing for Paradise lost, the hermit wants to reach a maturity of faith that will make the full revelation of Christ possible in his life. Therefore, he is determined to achieve a spiritual inner transparency that will allow God's love for the world to shine through him. This fullness of God's love is expressed in the divine plan of renewing all things in Christ. The glory of Christ must therefore be evident and visible in the hermit's every action: in his living and his dying.

Awakening

The question of the hermit's calling is, by implication, a question of love. The essence of love relates directly to life and death, to our hopes, expectations, and longings. When we ask about love, we ask about Christ, because it is through Him that the ultimate power of love is revealed through his tearing open the veil of suffering, agony, and death.

Love calls for awakening, and the hermit awaits this time of "his" love. There is an appointed time for everything under heaven: a time for joy and a time for sorrow, for spring and fall, for sunrise and sunset. There is also an appointed time for love, for which we have to mature patiently. Though we cannot make it come sooner, we should not oversleep

---

[19]   Saint John of the Cross, *Living Flame of Love*, 1.3 (New York, 1991).

our "appointment with love". Everybody has his own *kairos*, which he should recognize and respond to. There is no way to produce or cause love to happen, and there are no "techniques" of loving others. If somebody insists there are "methods" of loving, he has obviously missed the meaning of love we discuss in this book. That is why the hermit does not try to use any mystical techniques of breathing, mantras, visualizations, or the tantra. He rather waits patiently for God to come to him at the appointed time.[20]

We cannot cause love to happen, but love can be awakened. People wake up to love in a relationship; the other person's face, a gift of love, activates our dormant ability to love. The person awakened to love longs for unity with the loved one. That unity overcomes a former sense of isolation, enabling them to know each other just by means of this very act of love. Such unity or co-presence makes us happy because it tears down a wall of separation. Our desire to be in community, to be with other people, is rooted in this uniting energy of love. Love is a common language not only of the human race, but also of the whole universe. It seems that the boundless energy of love was the source of power for all those great saints who mastered the art of communication with animals and trees. Paulo Coelho writes about the power of love:

> At that moment, it seemed to him that time stood still, and the Soul of the World surged within him. When he looked into her dark eyes, and saw that her lips were poised between a laugh and silence,

---

[20] Cf. W. Johnston, *Życie w miłości: Modlitwa chrześcijańska w praktyce* (Cracow, 1997), pp. 145ff. See also William O. Johnston, *Being in Love: The Practice of Christian Prayer* (San Francisco, 1989).

> he learned the most important part of the language
> that all the world spoke – the language that
> everyone on earth was capable of understanding
> in their heart. It was love. Something older than
> humanity, more ancient than the desert. Something
> that exerted the same force whenever two pairs of
> eyes met, as had theirs here at the well. She smiled,
> and that was certainly an omen – the omen he had
> been awaiting, without even knowing he was, for
> all his life. The omen he had sought to find with
> his sheep and in his books, in the crystals and in
> the silence of the desert. It was the pure Language
> of the World.[21]

Love is thus related to a process of self-offering and a striving for unity, a truth that applies to all our relationships: as with people, so with God. When we meet God, we need to entrust ourselves unconditionally to His love. The hermit's life, at its most basic, aims to drown itself in God's love. In our life of faith there comes a time when God awakens our awareness of His overwhelming power of love. Such an awakening happens at the time of our first meeting with the Face of the Other. Although initially such an encounter can cause fear and uneasiness, gradually it becomes the only motive for the hermit's actions. Meeting the Face of the Unknown is what stimulates and strengthens the hermit in his everyday search for God. Meeting God's love enables us to open our hearts fully and to accept the Word prepared for us. So in faith, from the depths of the human spirit, comes a call, a yearning for the depths of God's mystery, and eventually

---

[21] Paulo Coelho, *The Alchemist* (Harper-Collins Publishers, 1995, 1999), p. 97.

He reveals a little bit of His glory that radiates from Christ's face.

Ecstasy

For the hermit, love means complete trust and a complete giving of self to God. In fact, every time we come face to face with authentic love, we find it has to do with experiencing ecstasy.[22] Ecstasy enters into a relationship when we offer ourselves to the loved one. Here living faith should be understood as being our answer given freely to a plentitude of grace granted to the humble. Nothing else but love makes the hermit change his way of life, directing it towards the Loved One. Love makes him "enter" the object of his love. Therefore, by loving unity, the hermit enters into the life of the Holy Trinity, which he now believes to be his own.

By loving God, the hermit arrives at a proper understanding of himself. By loving God simply and sincerely, he walks upon the path of self-knowledge. The more we are as one with Christ, the closer and more intimate our relationship with Him becomes, the more we can learn to understand our original identity. Such an encounter is a kind of "love game" between a human and God. We get to know ourselves thanks to our relations with God, the world, and other people. Each conversion is, as it were, a transition from the state of being foreign to oneself to a position of knowing one's identity in Christ. Love lets us know our identity, which guarantees our freedom.

---

[22] Cf. W. Hryniewicz, OMI, *Zarys chrześcijańskiej teologii Paschalnej*, vol.3: *Pascha Chrystusa w dziejach człowieka i wszechświata* (Lublin, 1991), pp. 148f.

The fervent love with which the hermit loves God can best be illustrated by a wedding, an image frequently used by many mystics. A person of faith knows the magnitude of the Gift he possesses. In accepting the Gift he simultaneously gives it back in an act of love to God and so to other people. In this way love can be extended to all of creation. Thus the hermit is open and ready to establish the ties of friendship and close relationships with other people. A mutual self-giving is not the exclusive privilege of marriage. It is possible wherever a human being has been awakened to simple, sincere, and selfless love. Everyone who has discovered a new life in Christ can now look at the world through His eyes. And it is at this moment when we forget ourselves, that we start living in Him. Now this is not I who live and love, but this is Christ who loves in me and through me.

Love is what puts all the difficult and dramatic moments of the hermit's life into the right perspective. Then every step brings us peace and every breath becomes a prayer animated by the Holy Spirit. The hermit's heart beats in accord with the Heart of all creation and that is why, somewhere deep within his mind, he can find a constantly renewing source of Love. All his creative and amazingly effective actions spring from that deep source, from that layer in the abyss of his existence, where he can see himself as the one who has been loved from the very beginning. In fact, the actions are no longer his own; as he is united with the Father, so his actions become God's, as He acts through him, with him, and in him (Jn 5:30).

IV

THE PRACTICE OF THE EREMITIC LIFE

As the Church cannot exist without martyrs, so it is impossible to conceive of the Church without those who live in solitude and who stand as testimony of the universal character of God's love. To understand not only the calling of the Apostles, but also the calling of each of the disciples, including the hermits, we have to understand the importance of Christ's gift of the Holy Spirit given in the context of the Paschal mystery. When St. Paul the Apostle attempts to explain how the Holy Spirit acts in our hearts and what the results are, he says that those led by the Holy Spirit are the children of God. Since it is not flesh nor the world but God who guides them, their lifestyle changes radically. In other words, everyone who has accepted the Paschal gift of the Spirit unites with the Giver and by his own life gives testimony to the truthfulness of the Gospel.

1. The Experience of Faith

Undoubtedly, the martyrs have a special place in the Church, mainly because of the testimony they have given to Christ and to His mission, a testimony so distinct and decipherable. However, the hermit's life, often called "a white martyrdom", is also a clear sign proclaiming the approach of the Kingdom, and so it is a gift to the Church community. The Church without hermits would have been, in a sense, incomplete and would have lacked the special presence of people devoted to one idea, which is searching for God in prayer, silence, solitude, and total simplicity of heart. The eremitic life is a constant and one-way pilgrimage of faith that leads the hermit in Christ's footsteps; that is why it always has the traits of a sacrifice offered on an altar of love.

The way of paradox

The hermit's life is full of different paradoxes and apparent contradictions. Some of them may surprise the hermit himself or even cause a certain uneasiness in him, not to mention others who look at his life from "outside". To many people who look at this way of life and want to be impartial observers of it, the eremitic experience of the desert seems to be an absurdity.

We have already mentioned above that the basic motive for choosing a solitary and silent life in a hermitage consists in an existential longing to meet and talk to God. The hermit chooses silence in order to enter fully into a dialogue; he chooses solitude in order to meet closely a personal presence. The way of the desert is thus not a stray and arid path, it does not lead to the negation of all the values of the world and of other people. Just the opposite: it is the way of mutual presence, dialogue, and friendship that shines where two freedoms and two hearts, divine and human, meet. The dialogue between the hermit and God means that two persons truly entrust themselves to each other in love, because unconditional trust is a necessary condition of every authentic dialogue.

For the hermit the gift of faith determines not merely the choice of the way of life, but also an elementary personal dynamism that enables him to go on and finish his journey successfully. The gift of faith makes it possible for us to open our hearts so that we are still better and better prepared to accept God, who wants to entrust Himself to us. Where faith is a dialogue, with two personal mysteries calling upon each other, God is the one who initiates the meeting, and the human respondent should only be obedient.

The silent word

What the eremitic life aims at is an inner, unifying meeting with God. Thanks to such a meeting, the hermit can understand better his existence. The hermit by an intuition of faith becomes aware that his calling makes no sense without Christ and His revelation. He learns that his dignity and the meaning of his life are clear and decipherable only in the context of proclaiming God's Kingdom. That is why the eremitic life means finding the meaning and goal of our life in Christ, who is the Word of God pronounced in history. That is faith. Here we can say that the dynamism of faith is always present where a simple and loving heart listens carefully to God's word pronounced still anew in the course of time. This word is so powerful and creative that it leads off and renovates the faith of a Christian, who as a result can participate in eternal things.

> The word of God is something alive and active:
> it cuts like any double-edged sword but more
> finely; it can slip through the place where the
> soul is divided from the spirit, or joints from the
> marrow; it can judge the secret emotions and
> thoughts. (Heb 4:12) [23]

In the hermit's life the experience of faith first means
to accept sincerely and fully the logic of the Gospel and to
reject everything that is contrary to it. In practice the things
to be rejected are all those schemes of thought that modern
rationalistic civilization cares for so much. Of course it
does not mean that faith neglects rational thinking, but it
introduces us to a new perspective of our existence, the world
and all its business. This new "optics" is based on a peaceful
and grace-given transition from the merely human trust
we place in other people to a trust we place in the invisible
reality of God. The very act of going to the desert puts all
the safety standards of the modern world in question. But the
significance of the desert would have been unclear if it had
not directed us to a different kind of logic, order, and world
– in other words, if it had not directed us to an absolute
mystery.

As a matter of fact, an authentic eremitic life is impossible
without a faith that is deep and mature. Only in faith can an
anchorite gradually discover his own religious identity, as well
as a new loving perspective of seeing God's presence in the
life of the individual and in the history of the world. Only
in faith can the hermit enter the deep way of the spiritual
life, where he takes all the radical requirements of the Gospel

---

[23] Cf. Hans Urs von Balthasar, *Prayer* (New York, 1961), pp. 27ff.

as his own, and where he becomes ready to accept all the consequences of his radical choices. By his decision for faith, the hermit rejects everything that is not related directly to Christ. Jesus is the One who is now the only and the ultimate value that serves as a standard for evaluating all the hermit's plans, thoughts, and decisions. That is why the words of St. Paul spoken to the Philippians become so dear to him:

> But because of Christ, I have come to consider all these advantages that I had as disadvantages. Not only that, but I believe nothing can happen that will outweigh the supreme advantage of knowing Christ Jesus my Lord. For him I have accepted the loss of everything, and I look on everything as so much rubbish if only I can have Christ and be given a place in him. I am no longer trying for perfection by my own efforts, the perfection that comes from the Law, but I want only the perfection that comes through faith in Christ, and is from God and based on faith. All I want is to know Christ and the power of his resurrection and to share his sufferings by reproducing the pattern of his death. That is the way I can hope to take my place in the resurrection of the dead. (Phil 3:7-11)

The hermit reproduces in faith and love the pattern of Christ's attitude towards the Father and the Holy Spirit, towards all people, and eventually towards the whole world. So, consequently, the hermit's spiritual search and the dialogue he holds with God make his Christian faith mature sooner and are a decisive factor in his true meeting with God, other people, and himself.

Faith, as a dynamism of grace and a personal direct relation to absolute mystery, brings us to God, who is not some theoretical assumption explaining the existence of the universe. Faith, which is a kind of special spiritual openness and sensitivity, brings us to Christ, who is the only true and possible direction and foundation of human existence. Thus, people who disregard living faith do not just strip themselves of important stimuli that could enliven their religious experience. In fact, their recognizing, accepting, and keeping faith in a loving God would be something much greater: it would determine their whole spiritual life as Christians. Here we can see how fundamental and unique a role faith plays in the Christian life.

Existential openness

Listening actively and carefully to the Word of God and adopting a certain existential attitude towards it are factors that determine how spiritually mature the hermit will grow on his solitary way of the desert. The eremitic life is a peaceful walking in the light of God's Word that is pronounced in the Church and addressed to each of us. The Eternal Word is full of endless potential for creativity, because it is still being pronounced from the depths of absolute Freedom. To listen to the Word means to believe in it. The attitude called faith is something very practical for the hermit: it enables him to give to the truth of God's word the first place in his life, before his subjective human views. By pondering over Holy Scripture the hermit can attain the proper attitude of listening, an attitude without which he cannot be authentic in his life and prayer.

Life in solitude can be described as a kind of journey towards Christ. Christ's love and faithfulness have become so clear and obvious for the hermit that now he feels obliged to give a personal and precise answer to them. So he wants to give an answer of faith that will spring from a "thinking heart". He also wants to give his answer, fully in the context of love, to the One whom he has entrusted his life and his future. In faith God is our future. So faith is the horizon of a meeting between the divine Word, so full and direct, and the human attitude of openness to the other. It is the horizon of a meeting between the divine piercing "straight through" and the human waiting "in front of".[24]

Faith is the way of Abraham who, having believed in God and His Word, dared to leave everything. In Abraham's example we can see a paradoxical dynamism of faith, so clear and distinct in the eremitic experience. The patriarch decides to take a chance and does not hesitate to make a sacrifice of his only son who was meant to be a blessing of the covenant.

Abraham's lifestyle, his way of thinking and acting, can be a great inspiration for the Christian hermit, because his faith was a kind of full and conscious openness to God (*capax Dei*), a kind of new sensitivity to the rays of God's revealing glory. Abraham, the Father of Nations, believed God just as much as he believed in God and that is why he was reckoned a righteous man. In other words, he believed and trusted God. He entrusted his whole life to his Lord and he did so contrary to any human logic or hope. The maturity of Abraham's faith can be seen especially in his openness to God's calling; he is ready to realize God's plans despite their being paradoxical

---

[24] Cf. T. Węcławski, op. cit., p. 58.

in the light of reasonable thinking. But if he had followed the logic of his reason, he would not have succeeded. The patriarch rejected the clear rules of reason in order to enter the dim realm of faith. He left everything in order to find a new quality of life, his life in God. Former emptiness was turned into the new fullness of God's covenant and promise (Gn 22:16-17).

The reality of covenant

Abraham's path of trust has set an example for the people of the desert throughout the centuries. Faith is a form of covenant, because in faith we accept the word and answer it actively. So faith contains both an element of spiritual death and an element of new birth to the life of grace. These are two basic elements of experiencing Passover; they determine the direction a solitary life should take. Faith requires us to reject our own tiny and particular truth and choose in favor of God's truth that we received in Christ. Abraham thus provides a model of faith for all the hermits, who in their spiritual life should care only for things that are eternal. To listen to the Word means to be obedient to it (*ob-audire*), which is to submit ourselves completely to the light of faith that we received. For the hermit, therefore, faith is not a mere rational acceptance of some "articles of faith". What it rather expresses is our real covenant with God and the complete trust we have in Him (*capax Dei*). He it is who is our ultimate destination. Building a close relationship with the Lord, Abraham expects to receive everything from Him, because the Lord keeps His promises.[25]

---

[25] *Catechism of the Catholic Church* (ed. 1994), paragraphs 26ff.

Through faith, the hermit can attain a fuller integrity of spirit and a more mature personality. Moreover, for him faith is the unique impulse to leave himself and to open and entrust his whole existence to the light of the Lord's glory. In order to develop a closer relationship with God, the anchorite has to face radical choices. The tension between two polarized options that he encounters is salutary, because it sets properly the course of his spiritual search. It means that there are moments when Christians have to stop minding their own business, get up and go out to meet the One whose calling they have heard and to whom they want to be faithful.

However, the hermit does not lose his own identity, he does not destroy the structure of his own self. Following the example of Abraham, the hermit gradually becomes ready and able to leave everything, including his very self, in order to take on a new kind of life, life in the Risen Lord. Such faith displays strong Paschal features and is closely related to the Resurrection and to the sending of the Holy Spirit to the community of disciples. The Spirit is the Spirit of the Father, the One who enables us to adhere with simplicity to the One God and to trust completely in His faithful (*emeth*) love.

Faith, as a covenant (*berit*) of love between God and man, means above all taking on an obligation to keep faith with each other, to care for each other, and to entrust one's life to the other. When we care for our friend, at every stage of our life we want to look out constantly for his ultimate good. The gift of the word makes the hermit see how much the Divine mercy cares for him.

What we have said should not lead us to the conclusion that in the hermit's life faith is founded on just giving a blind consent, with disregard for the light of reason. It is just the opposite: the arguments of reason are priceless for faith. The ancient rule that can be found in the thought of St. Augustine and St. Anselm is still true and valid today: *Crede ut intelligas* ("Believe so you can understand"). Firstly, faith means being open to the spring of grace; secondly, it means assuming the obligation to learn and understand grace in humility. The hermit knows that the spring of faith can gush for him only if he maintains his relationship with a mystery that exceeds any possible range of human understanding. On the one hand, we need to make every kind of intellectual effort to come closer to that mystery. On the other hand, we have to remember that our theological search will be effective only in proportion to the relationship of faith that develops between us and God.

2. The Eremitic Consecration

The hermit's faith expresses itself in his fervent desire to be consecrated. Of course, taking vows is not the only and mandatory way to fulfill the evangelical counsels and to be an authentic hermit. There are many examples in the history of eremitism that prove that beyond doubt. However, the commitment to follow the Gospel, which the hermit undertakes, seems to be much more clear and visible when he takes it in the form of vows.

The synthesis of the Gospel

When the hermit decides to be consecrated, he does not do so so much in order to secure himself from the many different perils of his difficult way. Rather he wants to express more distinctly his calling's character and value for the whole Church. The evangelical counsels are a specific synthesis of Christ's Good News, intended to encourage us to choose God's Kingdom definitely and with our whole selves. Through his consecration and thanks to the special charism he has been anointed with, the hermit abandons himself to his decision to follow in the footsteps of our Teacher and Master.[26]

> The stable pact that binds the hermit to the Lord inserts him deeply in the Paschal mystery, which is a death that leads to the resurrection. The vow thus conceived arouses an impulse of love that spurs the hermit to conform his whole existence to the demands of the Gospel or rather to Jesus Himself, model of chastity, poverty, and obedience.[27]

Thanks to the radical renunciation of basic goods that is related to professing the evangelical counsels, the hermit can more clearly show the true value of creation to the whole world, as well as to himself. The value has a personal character, which is the Trinitarian mystery of love revealed in Christ. Through his consecration, the hermit imitates Christ's purity, poverty, and obedience and makes them present in the Church. Thus Christ's virtues are made present, so to speak, in a "sacramental" way, because they become visible and effective. Where the hermit's consecrated way of life imitates the life and mission of Jesus Himself, the evangelical counsels seem to be a special sign of the love and holiness of the whole Church.

---

[26] Cf. J. Gogola, *Rady ewangeliczne* (Cracow, 1999), pp. 13f.
[27] *Constitutions,* op. cit., p. 5.

For the hermit, the path of the evangelical counsels has a mainly positive character. The hermit enters it joyfully, driven by an original impulse of love that urges his human heart to accept wholly and sincerely the message of the Good News to the point of consecration. Therefore, to enter the path of the evangelical counsels means to have a humble wish to follow in the footsteps of the Lord and to accept all the unforeseeable consequences of such a decision.

What the hermit looks for in his consecration is God, revealing Himself in the real and historical Person of Jesus. The hermit's way is Jesus and the concrete signposts of the Good News of the Kingdom are the evangelical counsels. Therefore, the counsels give direct access to the essence of the Gospel that, in fact, is Jesus Himself, His very Person and His deeds done in the name of the Father. When the Christian anchorite tries to practice the counsels, he is surprised to see that they are, like Jesus Himself, a point where the principal directions of God's redeeming plan intersect. Virginity gives freedom of the heart, so it supports us in loving God and creation. Poverty enables us to concentrate fully on following in Christ's footsteps and, at the same time, it makes us sensitive to the many different needs of other people. Obedience has a formative value and it builds in us a sense of universal human equality and solidarity.

The power of the charism

Undoubtedly, the way of the evangelical counsels, and even the very opportunity of entering it, seems to be one of the greatest gifts the hermit has received. Gradually he sees more and more clearly that his very decision to be consecrated, as well as his everyday practice of the vows he has taken, are all a gift from the Father who is the only source of any grace. Since thus committing oneself by vows to the practice of evangelical counsels presupposes a charism, taking such vows must be a matter of God's choice and good pleasure, and it has nothing to do with purely human effort or initiative. The grace of such vows is related directly to the greatest charism of the Christian life, to love. It is thanks to love that the hermit remembers why his life has been distinguished by suffering and service, which are marks granted not for collecting more personal merits, but in order to give glory to God and to work for the good of the Church and the whole world.

Thanks to his consecration, the hermit step by step makes true in his life those words about being the light of the world that is not to be put under a bushel, but on a lampstand. Indeed, the hermit's calling is rather paradoxical, which causes a good deal of suffering for him. On the one hand, he is called to solitude, but on the other hand, he must bear witness to God's Kingdom to countless people. This only seems to be a contradiction. Its ultimate meaning and value become clear to the hermit over the course of his life. The contradiction can be understood only in the context of the Trinitarian mystery. The mystery of an inner exchange of love that constantly overflows in the bosom of the Trinity is on the one hand secret and silent, but on the other hand it initiates historical Revelation and the redeeming mission of the Son and the Holy Spirit. According to Origen, God is simultaneously the Silent One, the One who speaks and the One who is spoken about.

The hermit also wants to see his mission between, so to speak, two extremes: between his solitary and hidden prayer and the testimony he gives to the world; between silence and the need to speak out. The hermit's life would have been torn to pieces and left miserably incomplete if he had tried to build it on the foundation of his own ideas. But fortunately the way of the desert is not his own invention, but a gift of the Holy Spirit. This Spirit, the unifying principle of the mutual relationships of the Holy Trinity, is also the source of unity and peace in the life of the hermit. For him, the land beyond the horizon of the Holy Spirit is "a wasteland", the dwelling place and kingdom of the demon; this "no man's land" fills him with a holy fear, not with terror.

Just as the Son of Man

Since the evangelical counsels flow directly from the very heart of Christ's life and teaching, they are of great help in our following His example in relating to the Father, to other people, and to the whole world. Each of the vows is a step on the way of imitating the Lord. Each of them expresses our special relation to Christ, who was consecrated and sent from the Father by the power of the Holy Spirit. He was rich but He became poor for our sake and chose the way of inner smallness up to the point of His crucifixion. Being free of spirit and undivided of heart, He loved all people unconditionally and without borders. Above all, He desired to fulfill the will of the Father with perfect obedience, by following the path of humility, suffering, and total trust.[28]

In the hermit's life the act of professing the evangelical counsels reflects the dynamism of love, still thirsting to be a fuller and more radical gift. Surely the vows are a sign of one's

---

[28] Cf. J. Gogola, op.cit., pp. 12ff.

striving for perfection and, at the same time, they induce inner maturity and the readiness to accept it. Since the hermit's consecration clears the way for spiritual development, it provides the unique conditions needed to strengthen his heart in the love of the Father through Christ, the Savior of the world. Love, embracing the whole of creation, tends to overcome any element of evil present in the world, which is to overcome the disorder of covetous desires. Love thus truly makes the hermit's heart broad, pure, and free.

Consecrated solitude has a Paschal character; it changes the hermit into a man of God. The hermit loves the world, but simultaneously in his pilgrimage to the land of the Promised Kingdom, he is able to overcome the world by entrusting it to the Creator. By the vows he has made, the hermit becomes "a prophet of freedom", a messenger of final liberation for all of humanity to whom he brings the Good News by means of being consciously useless to the world. By his consecration the hermit renounces everything that is unimportant and trivial, and so he becomes a sign of contradiction against the slavery of fashion, social structures, conventions, and public opinion. Walking his way, he seeks out his own identity and gives his personal testimony of how to fight persistently for our human dignity.

3. The Necessity of Discipline

The hermit has only one educator: the Holy Spirit. In the school of the *Paraclete* he learns step by step how to be humble and wise, how to accept the Spirit's gifts of harmony and peace. It does not mean at all that the hermit disregards the advice of a wise spiritual guide, but just the opposite:

such advice plays a decisive role in the hermit's life. In his life's pilgrimage the hermit learns how to decipher priceless inner inspirations in the light of "outward" advice. Whether the inner light comes from his own heart or from an advisor, what the hermit always longs for is a wise attitude of being obedient to God's grace.

Learning to serve the Lord

The hermit's inner discipline forms his spiritual sensitivity and openness toward the approaching word. Discipline is an everlasting lesson that applies to the hermit's whole spiritual journey. Is it not surprising that even after years of experience, he still needs to retain his first zeal for learning? Only the burning zeal for spiritual development, accessible to those of simple and pure hearts, makes it possible to progress in self-discipline in the school of love. But how can an elderly man retain an agile mind and the clear eye of a child? Why do most people stop learning right after the end of their school years, if in fact they learned anything during them at all? How can one keep the mind of a child, bright and awake, throughout the whole of one's life? Is it at all possible?

The hermit approaches this problem, like all others, in a very practical manner. It poses a challenge for him, which he wants to respond to. The answer he finds comes from the Scriptures, and what it says is that in order to retain the childlike attitude of spirit, the hermit must let the child be born in him. To form oneself in the way of the desert means to discover the child's face within. Submitting to discipline is nothing else but adopting an attitude that opens our spiritual eyes to the light of grace. The light of God's eternal grace is accessible only to a child's eyes, with their innocent and thoughtful look. The hermit has always had spiritual eyes, but they have stayed closed, which means useless. He does not even have the slightest idea how to open them. Therefore he humbly asks "the Lord of all that is impossible" to help him open his spiritual eyes, so that he can see the beauty of the Lord.

The wise and delicate approach the hermit takes to himself and to other people is called discipline. It gives a solid foundation for developing all the virtues. Each of the virtues reaches its culmination in love, which is openness toward God, other people, and the world. Love, as a continuous exchange of what is our supreme personal value, comes from the realm of the Trinity. The life of God, dynamic as it is, wishes to manifest itself in a real human relationship, so it requires a pure heart and a spirit that is transparent to the rays of eternal love. Such spiritual transparency can be achieved only in cooperation with the Lord in the way of maintaining self-discipline: in other words, in the school of God's love.

Three pillars of spirituality

Silence is the first pillar of eremitic rigor. It is a basic condition for opening our hearts to the light of contemplation. Silence, being a grace, provides us with a great opportunity to change our hearts and to entrust our spirit to the Lord. Between the hermit's silence and the word of his Master there is a dynamic harmony of faith, the harmony of an intense relationship. For the hermit silence is the simplest way to accept and understand the affairs of the Lord and His Kingdom.

To start practicing the virtue of silence is to limit our speech wisely and therefore to take control of all levels of our personality. But silence is also something more than a mere absence of words. In fact, silence is an attitude of the heart that is obedient to God's Word. It is a kind of atmosphere the hermit wants to dwell in and a kind of energy that enables him to listen more carefully and to be more sensitive to every single aspect of God's presence in his everyday life. Therefore, silence is related to our inner sensitivity, to our heart's intuition that unifies us with absolute freedom. The gift of silence thus becomes the gift of an intimate dialogue.

Silence, so understood, is an introduction to a contemplative dialogue of prayer, in which the word and deep silence alternate with each other. The human being, amazed with the light of God's glory, becomes silent and lets the Word settle in the depths of his heart. The Word reveals an eternal "song of silence" ringing at the bosom of the Trinity, a "song of silence" that has, so to speak, its fluctuations and breathes with an interpersonal melody of love. The silent word, which speaks by the power of its very presence, teaches the hermit a new language that can be called a "fortitude of being". It reveals new horizons and shows new abilities of the human word that can find its greatest meaning only in connection with the absolute truth of God.

In eremitic spirituality silence does not exclude speaking and does not discount meetings and dialogues. What is aimed at is bringing harmony between the heart and the mind, between the spirit and the body, and eventually between God and man. Silence sets us free from the burden of words that are banal and meaningless, from a humdrum that disturbs the true essence of the word. A human word, when it comes from the deep silence of the heart, causes a creative anxiety in everyone who listens to it. It becomes the word of a prophet, proclaiming eternity.

The rigor of solitude – the second pillar of eremitic ascesis – does not mean escaping and isolating oneself, and it is not misanthropy of any kind. The hermit wants to meet and confront himself in solitude in order to identify his heart's deceitfulness and to get rid of it. The choice to live in solitude is surely the choice to leave the humdrum of the worldly marketplace, but the character of such a decision is not negative. The hermit does not aim at running away from the world and its affairs and at finding a safe shelter somewhere there in the wilderness. It is not right to consider him a fearful and frustrated fellow, a runaway who is afraid of confronting his self. Solitude has nothing to do with existential neurosis, but it is rather a creative search for the flame of love that burns in God's heart.

Among many different ways in which mystics illustrated the realm they encountered, the realm of God, there are several descriptions of desert, silence, and solitude. The terms used in the school of negative theology suit well the sense of the eremitic rigor of solitary life. Such a life can be characterized by a polarized tension. Existential solitude teaches us how to overcome the limitations of our own weakness. By freeing himself from his pride, vanity, and any other kind of inner disorder, the hermit comes closer to the state of spiritual solitude, which is a tranquil and expectant openness of heart. Such openness leads us to the other stage of solitude, which is a transition from our natural point of view to a divine and absolute perspective, a transition from ourselves to God. Therefore, the rigor of solitude seems to be related to the fullness of God's truth, and the anchorite is not exposed to the danger of just minding himself and his own business.

What occupies the center between the two extremes we described is the existential solitude of God Himself. This is what the human heart wants to absorb and this is where it wants to rest. The eremitic solitude is in no case a fruitless and spiritually empty isolation, a cold indifference toward people and the world or a selfish passiveness. Just the opposite, it is a space of redemption, full of spiritual life and meant to accept and change any human distress, sorrow, or fear. The dialectical tension between the time of spiritual purification and the attitude of openness toward the Transcendent One can eventually be eased by the gift of Presence and Meeting. Such a gift introduces us to a new relationship and a new life that can develop in our solitary, silent, and free spirit. Solitude remains the only space where the encounter of the two freedoms and the two mysteries is possible; now solitude turns out to be the fullness of life.

Fasting, prayer, and almsgiving build the third pillar of the eremitic rigor that helps to develop the spiritual life. When Jesus teaches His disciples these practices, He takes fasting, prayer, and almsgiving out of their Judaic legal context. He points out that they are valuable only if practiced in solitude, because only then are they free from worldly concerns and hypocrisy. For the hermit fasting does not taste like a hardship, but it is rather the entrance to a heavenly joy. It makes the human body pure and more spiritual and elevates the human heart in prayer to the Lord. The hermit does not live on bread alone, but on every word that comes from the mouth of God. It is, above all, the power of the

Word that gives him inner happiness. Fasting therefore seems to teach the lesson of putting ourselves in God's hands, and it leads us to change our lives and to bear the fruit of humility and trust.[29]

For the hermit, fasting means encountering God's Kingdom present in his heart. It has nothing to do with sentimental emotions, but it is rather a manifestation of the power of God's grace acting in the human spirit. Fasting thus is not just abstaining from food, but it is also curbing one's thoughts, desires, and feelings. Its meaning goes deeply into the intimate spheres of the human spirit, which we have called "a pure heart". Fasting shows itself to be a joyful attitude of body and spirit, enabling the hermit to make a constant effort of prayer peacefully. We cannot expect our spiritual life to develop fully into a form of mystical prayer without reaching inner peace and without engaging all the energy we have.

4. Hermitage

There is nothing more necessary for, and characteristic of, the hermit than to remain constantly in his hermitage. The hermitage is the determined space of the hermit's experience, which is marked by solitude, silence, prayer, and fasting. Each of those elements we can relate to any form of the Christian life, and each of them seems to be necessary for the spiritual development of every Christian. The hermitage, though, is what makes solitude, silence, prayer, and fasting

---

[29] Cf. A. Grün, *Fasten – Beten mit Leib und Seele* (Münsterschwarzach: Vier-Türme-Verlag, 1984), chapter 4; quoted after A. Grün, *Post* (Cracow, 1991), p. 33.

the characteristic signs of the hermit's life. The hermitage's walls and garden, as well as its whole austere beauty, add a specific flavor to the hermit's life.

Austere simplicity

Therefore, nothing is more suitable and necessary for the hermit than to remain in the cell. It is the space where his faith and love grow and where he tries ever anew to find his lost God. The path where he looks for Christ is none other than the path determined by the solitude and recollection of his heart. The solitude of his hermitage is what feeds the fertile soil of his inner concentration.

The only adornment of the cell is its simplicity, poverty, or a kind of austere beauty. Any luxury and all that could become for the hermit a motive for distraction or for attachment should be utterly foreign to it. The hermit strives to make poverty his dwelling's only ornamentation. Modesty, simplicity, and poverty constitute the core of the eremitic rigor and, at the same time, they reveal the natural beauty of things. Here is a place of prayer and a room for rest and work free from all that is redundant. When we progress on the way of self-abandonment and inner smallness, we consequently want to get rid of all our possessions that are redundant and a burden to us.

The cell is a place for work, reading, eating, and rest, but all those occupations make sense only because it is, above all, a place of prayer. The hermit chooses the solitude of his cell in order to intensify his prayer, which often becomes a dramatic struggle. While in his cell, having fled far from any preoccupations, the hermit fixes the eyes of his soul on God, and with a simple and pure heart he entrusts all his cares to the Lord. Knowing that the cell is a special place, which God has chosen for him, the hermit grows there spiritually so as to attain inner wisdom, understanding, and peace. He withdraws from worldly business and keeps watch in order to devote himself to holy and diligent "idleness", which means a contemplative attitude of faith.

The cell provides a unique possibility to be in touch with the living Word of God, which affords the opportunity to know Christ better, and which immerses us in His limitless wisdom. For several hours of every day and night the hermit gives himself up to *lectio divina* in order to encounter the Word, which is so deep and dynamic. Spiritual reading is not just studying text, but it is also a starting point for meditating on the essence of Divine Revelation. The heart that meditates can be better prepared to recognize the voice of God Who approaches, and Who is the only Guide in the mysterious paths of salvation.

Corporal works are ordered to the effort of meditation. That is why the meditating hermit prefers simple manual occupations to any intellectual activities. Manual work provides the human spirit with an opportunity to relax and rest, and what is more, when performed with due care, it can be a natural base for the human spirit to ascend to the Lord. For the hermit occupied with simple physical work, it is not difficult to keep his spirit calm. By weaving mats and baskets or assembling rosaries the hermit controls the fluctuation of thoughts and allows his heart to remain united with God without his mind becoming tired.

A holy place

Therefore, for the hermit the cell is a holy place. It is a horizon where the Father, still reaching out to meet us, reveals His elusive presence. When God invites us to a deeper level of contemplative prayer, He asks for complete inner silence and peace; faithful perseverance in the cell is the best means to achieve such a disposition. Through constant effort and labor the hermit gradually forgets himself, leaves behind all his fears and worries, and feels an overwhelming desire to love the Lord.

> Hasten then to overcome your passions, so that admitted to the King's intimacy you may cling to Him as to an intimate friend. Let the eye of your mind be fixed on the Author of light. That eye will be all the purer the less it will be veiled by the mist of phantasms and vain thoughts.[30]

The cell is therefore a place where the hermit grows and matures to the last things, to eternity. To settle there is always a solemn and decisive moment for him. Entering the cell seems to attract and, at the same time, to scare him, because it inevitably means the absence of any other people. However, the severity and simplicity of the cell can be attractive only to a person with a rich interior life. Living in the cell, holy and pure as it is, seems to be the best kind of eremitic discipline and formation.

The cell is the best teacher for him who dwells

---

[30] St. Peter Damian, *Opusculum 25;* quoted after *Constitutions of the Congregation of the Camaldolese Hermits of Monte Corona* (Bloomingdale, Ohio, 1994), p. 12.

long in it, and as time goes on it teaches with
action what the tongue of flesh cannot express
with the sound of words. Let the brother persevere
alone in the cell, which will teach more fully him
who dwells there how he ought to live.[31]

So, the cell is not only a place of rest, peace, and prayer,
but also a dramatic scene where two freedoms, human and
divine, interact with each other. While locked in the cell the
hermit finds anew his old desires and he longs again to be
with other people. The hermit is not a soldier of fortune, nor
a tourist ever looking for beautiful new places. What his life
can be illustrated by is rather the pilgrim nomad, who does
not look behind and spares no effort in his "struggle with the
desert". The cell throws out everybody who is so weak as to
rely on himself. Only a person who prays humbly, relies on
the power of grace, and looks for solutions and support solely
in God can persevere in the cell.

The continuous dwelling in the cell seems to be not
only a basic element of the hermit's experience, but also
an important factor in his sanctification; the cell is like a
crucible where the hermit's heart is tested like gold. Above
all, it is the lesson of humility that the solitude of the cell
imparts to us. Freed from distractions that blind the mind,
the hermit begins to see himself in the light of God's glory.
Encountering the light of grace lets him take the measure of
his own emptiness, weakness, and imperfection. The more
deeply and harshly the hermit experiences his own misery
and insufficiency, so much the more intense and profound
will be his prayer and the confidence he has in God.

---

[31] St. Peter Damian, *Opusculum, 15, 18* (ibid.).

Stay in your cell as in paradise, St. Romuald advised his disciples, he who knew very well that the cell was also a battlefield and a place of ascetic efforts. The hermit is, most of all, endangered by idleness and *acedia*, which is listlessness with regard to things of the Spirit.

> The hermits consequently must take great care, as the holy Fathers have taught, to be always engaged, so that the devil may always find them occupied and not be able to find a moment in which to tempt them. Let each one endeavor to attend with care and interest to manual labor at opportune and determined hours; at other hours, on the contrary, let him dedicate himself to reading and prayer as well as to other disciplines of the soul either with spiritual or with bodily exercises, so that every moment of the day and night seems to him short and insufficient. Each one should act in such a way that he has more things to do than time in which to do them.[32]

A wise hermit still guards his cell against the pressure of worldly and humdrum information by avoiding the disorders of reading newspapers, excessive correspondence, and visits. He should always remember that the cell is constituted by the lack of changing voices and pictures and, above all, the lack of another human being. The cell offers the hermit an abundant sphere of freedom, and therefore it provides him with a perfect spiritual atmosphere to follow in Christ's footsteps in solitude and silence. The cell, at least potentially, opens up the possibility of approaching and contemplating all

---

[32] Cf. *Constitutions*, op. cit., p.11.

the mysteries of the life of Jesus. Eventually, the cell appears to be a sign of devoting ourselves radically to the search for God and His glory. It is here that the source of the hermit's peace and confidence can be found. With the support of the Holy Spirit's gifts, the hermit meets in his cell the One who is his way and his life.

5. Work

One of the most marvelous things that the hermit can enjoy is an attitude of gentleness and gratefulness. Progressing on the way of silence he realizes how good and holy are all things, because they can be originally related to the source of all creation, which is God. The hermit unceasingly gives thanks to Christ for the gift of life, which each of us should constantly care for and develop. The attitude of gratefulness comes from realizing that the whole world, delicate and fragile as it is, is a great and good treasure that the Creator has deposited in our hands. The goodness of the world seems to be not only a gift, but also a task to be undertaken by means of human labor.

On behalf of the renewal

If we want to live the eremitic life maturely and responsibly, so rich in forms as it can be, we cannot aim at cultivating our own individual conceptions, projects, or ideas, nor at fulfilling our individual needs or tasks. Not in order to achieve his own perfection does the hermit set out on his solitary voyage. On the contrary, he considers his way and mission to be a part of a great common effort to change and renew the cultural and spiritual life of humanity. Therefore, the eremitic life seems to be one of those underlying factors that really influence the social structures so that people can fruitfully work and multiply the common material and spiritual good. The hermit does not want – and in fact is not even able – to separate himself from the concrete experiences of modern people: from touching the toil, conflicts, and struggles they face. He takes part in all those experiences just because, through his existential meeting with Christ, he gains a new perspective and a new sensibility, and so he becomes even more open to all the problems of the modern world.

So, we can hardly take a hermit for a person who limits his entire mission to a few prayers he recites and to some daily routines necessary in everyday life. The hermit has to take into account all the difficult problems endangering the world today. But the hazards the modern world faces, which cause fear and can bring about a catastrophe of culture and civilization or even the total annihilation of mankind, do not paralyze his activity to improve the world. It is just the opposite: realizing how deeply he is rooted in the life of society and how greatly responsible he should be for the world and its future, the hermit wants to take part in coping with the difficulties and anxieties of today.

Of course, the hermit is much more a person of prayer than a person of activity, but he is far from neglecting any creative action towards changing the world for the better. When he undertakes a task, he does not aim at performing a great many actions for an immediate and striking effect. He is not an activist who lives on organizing neurotically different actions and events that are in fact inspired by his inner chaos and anxiety. The hermit strongly opposes misdirected work, which aspires only to achieve success, domination, prestige, and fame, and which can easily destroy other people's good.

There is nothing more foreign to the hermit than the clownery of a glittering career, success, and all those vulgar illusions that tempt the modern world. For the hermit, his work is one of elementary and daily activities, necessary for his own sanctification as well as for the sanctification of the world. It is not a mere object, money-maker, and article of trade, but it is rather a way of realizing his life's calling and approaching his life's fulfillment. Thus the hermit becomes a sign of protest against all the vulgar tendencies of modern civilization, which view work only in terms of productivity and money. Such a way of thinking, and consequently of acting, testifies to how much worldly affairs have degenerated and have gone far astray from what would be a humanitarian and harmonious course of events.

A sense of activity

If human work is to use human abilities and talents in a wise and proper way, and if it is going to build up the good of the person and society, it should be performed in an atmosphere of love. Therefore the primary motivation for any activity consists in the human desire to serve individuals and society. Our work should not be motivated by our own or our family's financial needs. The hermit works because the work is his calling. Through his work he not only makes use of his talents but, above all, he expresses his freedom and his love of God and of people.[33]

Only when we see work in such a manner can we get

---

[33] Cf. Thomas Merton, *Life and Holiness* (New York, 1963), pp. 121ff.

satisfaction, joy, and a sense of personal fulfillment from our activity. Work, when performed wisely and seen as an expression of human, love-motivated solidarity and service, turns out to be a very concrete way of liberation. The freedom we win, in the course of our daily chores that we fulfill wisely and conscientiously, is not abstract, but real and tangible. Here freedom means throwing away our burden of frustration and anxiety and getting rid of the destructive feeling of being lost in life. So on the one hand, it is a freedom *from* a devastating fear; but on the other, it is a kind of openness *toward* all the creative, vital, and beautiful elements of human experience. In other words, it is a freedom at the service of love.

The hermit prays unceasingly while he works. The work he offers to God consists of both the labor of his spirit and the labor of his hands. His work becomes a form of prayer, especially when it is related to a physical task undertaken in answer to God's calling. In any human activity performed with a view to changing creatively the world for the better, there are ever prayers and actions, spirit and body, that constantly interchange and cooperate with each other. All the occupations of the hermit are meant to make his body governed by the law of human work and to keep his spirit fit. Following the example of the Holy Family of Nazareth, the hermit, by doing his daily chores tries to sanctify the world and to put created things at the service of the contemplative life – and all this for the greater glory of God.

> Whatever manual labor that you do, inside or outside the cell, always do it meditating on the law of the Lord or singing the divine canticles as a relief of fatigue. During work nothing prevents

prayer, and this is not at all useless. On the contrary, only one prayer, made in the fear of God, in liberty of spirit and with radiant countenance by one who labors is more easily accepted than ten thousand prayers of one who despises manual labor through laziness or negligence.[34]

The creative character of love

It seems that the dynamism of the hermit's activity is born out of his creative passion to multiply the good in the world, a passion that is a fruit growing from the soil of prayer. The hermit sees his life in terms of goodness and beauty, so for him to participate wisely in the course of everyday matters means to be a kind of artist. In his trying to live a creative life, the hermit immerses all the occupations of his hands and mind in the impetuous river of God's love. He knows by experience that we cannot live a creative and beautiful life unless we love; anyway, only love can be truly creative, only love can light up our lives with joy and fulfillment. Contemplative prayer is practically the only realm where we fully realize how abundant and lavish are God's wisdom and love in the entire universe. Here is the point where two spheres of the eremitic experience, prayer and action, come together. That is why contemplation seems to be a foundation of all the hermit's actions, which, thanks to it, gain the traits of harmony, balance, and proportion.

The hermit sees his work in its supernatural and redemptive dimension, because he sees it in relation to the person and the deeds of Christ. The work, performed in

---

[34] Blessed Paul Giustiniani, *Rule*, 86; quoted after: *Constitutions*, p. 44.

the wisdom of the Word and in the power of the Spirit, is included in the Paschal mystery, which is a creative energy of change. To meet the Crucified and Risen Lord in the Paschal mystery means to see the hermit's life and work in a new light. The way in which the hermit engages himself in the matters of the world and the way he undertakes efforts to make God's kingdom come into being on earth is somehow similar to the Paschal pains of redemption. The work seen in its Paschal dimension is not free from hardships and even suffering, because it is meant to be a kind of gift and sacrifice. The salvation and redemption we enjoy through Christ's work of salvation do not ease the hardships of our work, but they reveal and explain the ultimate meaning of human toil.

By putting the hardships of his work in the perspective of the Paschal sacrifice, the hermit allows his earthly actions to be enlivened with the rays of grace that emanate from the Risen Lord. That is why hermits are so unbelievably creative and effective in approaching and fulfilling ever-new tasks. Hermits are people exceptionally gifted with many different charisms, abilities, and talents, which make the fruits of their work lasting and universal.

Having all those gifts at his disposal, the hermit wants to use them creatively and fruitfully, so he puts himself at the disposal of God and other people. The forms of the hermit's engagement are many and diverse, while the subjects of his engagement are rich and profound. His great passion for love and the talents he possesses turn his work into a tool that he uses for serving God, other people, and the world. He acts carefully, reliably, and soberly, free from any desire for personal success and from indulging his vanity.

As we have already said, the hermit's work and the way

he approaches it have nothing to do with his aspirations for an individual perfection or with ignoring the social context of his efforts. One of the main aims of modern hermits consists in improving the social consciousness of people, in strengthening their sense of their own dignity, responsibilities, and rights.

The same applies to human work and the place it should properly have in the life of an individual and the life of a community. Here the hermit should also be the evangelical "leaven" and a source of inspiration for changes, occurring not only in the individuals who want to take his advice but also in social structures.

Undoubtedly, the task is Herculean, and it refers to the entirety of human life and to all the spheres of human experience: politics, the economy, business, international relations, the whole realm of culture and civilization. Compared to them though, the works of the hermit may seem to be unbelievably trifling, not to say laughable. However, the way of the desert is not quixotic, but fully evangelical in its logic, and we have to stress that the divine logic often looks paradoxical to human eyes. The hermit wants to relate all his efforts to the parable of the mustard seed that, tiny as it is, grows and bears fruit according to the wise plan of God. From the moment of Christ's Incarnation human work has gained a new, supernatural dimension. Now human work participates in the great transformation of the universe that has been going on from the time the Word became flesh and power was revealed in weakness.

6. The Dynamism of Struggle

While the desert is where God shows His glory and while it is a place of Revelation, it is also a land demons like to visit. Christ Himself witnessed it because it was He whom the devil tempted severely in the wilderness. Of course, the hermit seeks a shelter in the desert in order to concentrate on the great silence of God. Simple and poor as he is, the hermit is led out into solitude not only for his own sake, but also for the sake of the whole of humanity. He knows well that his mission consists in listening and transferring what he heard and understood to other people.

The shadow of temptation

However, the hermit is wise enough to remember that he will not avoid meeting Satan. He cannot be sure how often and how intensely he is going to confront the devil, but he knows that the struggle will inevitably come. The hermit's experience of temptation is really manifold, but the attitude he always displays in the face of such a struggle is submission to the dispositions of Divine Providence, because it is God who permits men to be tempted. Every such trial, if he undergoes it successfully, strengthens his faith and love. Christ wants His disciple to have trust only in Him and to act supported solely by His Grace. That is why He permits all those hardships and satanic attacks to happen.

It is really difficult to foresee all the tricks Satan may use in order to hurt and finally destroy the hermit. Evil can act delicately, imitating closely God's subtle presence. On the other hand, when he does not have any other access to a saintly person, he can openly launch an attack with all his brutality. Then the desert becomes a place of horror. The hermit feels as if he is beset and tied up with no help from anybody. He experiences strong temptations; the ground is cut out from under his feet and all the lights that guided him before are gone.

Those terrible feelings become even stronger at night, when prayer seems to be practically impossible and when his eyes are too wide open to sleep. At such moments his heart is terrified, and it experiences horrible emptiness and total loss; God seems to be lost too. The hermit feels that his staying in the wilderness is a complete absurdity, he starts asking what he is here for and why he is so mad as to stay at this place even a short while longer. In fact, all his thoughts, feelings, and desires concentrate on finding a way out, and the sooner, the better.

The time of temptation can be prolonged on and on, or on the contrary, it can cease suddenly and change into a time of rest and peace. It depends only on the plans of Divine Providence. The moment the anxiety, the sense of loss, the darkness, the suffering, and the panic begin, it is a clear sign that the time of spiritual struggle and the time of devilish traps is approaching. The evil spirit can use our senses, emotions, mind, body, or soul for his tricks. He can suddenly fill the cell with his presence – as a luminous angel or as an angry beast. Under the guise of good inspirations the devil can tempt the hermit to undertake heroic deeds, and under the mask of spiritual wisdom he can tempt him to set out on a missionary journey and to start teaching people. Moreover, in order to make his suggestions credible, the devil will surely use coherent logical arguments and he will even quote the Scriptures.

It seems that the person faced with such a strong attack has no chance at all. It also seems that apparently he is completely disarmed and has nothing to support him in the battle. He is not able to pray, meditate, or read the Scriptures in order to calm his thoughts and heart. It seems like earth and heaven have made a pact against the hermit's poor soul. But even then there is a way out, a chance for victory: the chance is to remain persistently and watchfully patient in the face of temptation. Persevering patiently in the time of temptation and praying for help to the Mother of God, even if our every word is heavy as stone, are the turning points of the spiritual struggle.

The power of patience

To persist patiently and trustfully during trial is really difficult. What we need to win the battle is great fortitude and spiritual experience. The patience displayed in time of suffering is the surest evidence of one's spiritual perfection and love of God and people. All other indications of Christian perfection may be called into doubt, but the faith kept with God in great physical and moral suffering testifies infallibly to the presence of the principal Christian virtues of faith and charity.

Only a childish or spiritually ignorant person can suppose that one can stay in the desert without experiencing temptation. It would be much better for such an ignorant person if he stayed safely at home and did not try to face solitude and temptation. But if he dares to do so, his only chance lies in acknowledging his own weakness and ignorance and in trusting God unconditionally like a child. Only God can support and save his life.

One of the greatest spiritual supports the hermit can receive is the grace of realizing that God is the only practical reference point for the human heart. It seems to be even more important when we bear in mind that the Christian hermit's mission is a charism that is a gift benefiting the Church and the whole world. The hermit always tries to remember that his mission, together with the suffering it entails and all his spiritual hardships and struggles, has a redemptive value for the whole of humanity. Staying in the silence of his cell, he focuses above all on other people. When he prays, he submits to the eremitic discipline. When he faces trials and temptations, he does it all as if in the name of humanity. By uniting himself with Christ, living in Him, through Him, and with Him, the hermit participates in the Lord's Passover.

In His Passover, Christ accepted torments out of the love that He has for each of us, with no exceptions and limits. The Paschal character of the hermit's life gives him a strong sense of solidarity with people all over the world. Hence, the eremitic mission, which is a gift for the individual, but also for the entire community of the Church, seems to be included in and united with the mission of Christ Himself. The hermit identifies his life with that of Christ – particularly with the mystery of Christ's Passion, which is the mystery of darkness and light, the mystery of humiliation and glory, the mystery of death and resurrection. The eremitic way is the way of the Passion, because the hermit cooperates with Christ for his own salvation and for the salvation of his brothers. The hermit dies and rises with the Lord not only in the sacrament of baptism, but also through the faith, hope, and love that he professes still anew every time he experiences a temptation.

The theological virtues become the signpost of his existence. Now he can put aside his old self, give up his old way of life, and gradually put on the Paschal self (*homo Paschalis*), whose way of life is to turn self into a gift to God and other people.[35]

On the way of his solitary journey the hermit encounters real evil, which God permits. Experiencing temptation and struggling with the powers of darkness, he should not be filled with fear but rather really careful and alert. As soon as the hermit sees the light of God, he also notices the shadow of the devil, an exceptionally envious and cunning creature. In any case, the demon will be a total loser, because of Christ's absolute victory. That is why through grace the hermit is free from the paralyzing fear of the devil. Guarding himself in dread of evil is no longer the priority of his life; just the opposite: what he cares most for now is keeping his heart open to the Trinitarian mystery of God that he wants to unite and identify with still more closely. The danger of temptation is no longer terrifying, because each of his new trials ends victoriously and brings the hermit's heart closer to the absolute mystery of God. However, as he bravely awaits his struggle with the devil he in no way puts the Lord his God to the test, because his courage results rather from the profound trust and faith he has put in his Savior.

Spiritual martyrdom

The ways of defeating the powers of evil are always the same: faith, fasting, prayer, and the Sign the of Cross. The means the hermit has at his disposal are the means of those

---

[35] Cf. W. Hryniewicz, op. cit., p. 57.

who are extremely poor (*anawim Jahwe*): faith, suffering, and prayer, which are very practical and effective in his life. The eremitic cell remains a school where he continuously learns God's love. There he grows in acceptance of the ultimate mystery, which can be seen only in the perspective of the Cross. By accepting the mystery the hermit accepts the power of the Lord, so Christ is now able to perform His great works in him. Thus the hermit comes closer to understanding what martyrdom is all about.

The hermit is probably not going to become a martyr in the strict sense of the word. However, he constantly prays for this grace and is ready to receive it. His martyrdom has a different meaning: it accompanies his offering himself up to God as a sacrifice, his putting aside his own self and leaving to meet the Lord whom he seeks, desires, and awaits. To put aside his own self and to overcome his own phobias, frustrations, longings, and all the inner anxiety of agitated emotions and thoughts – this is the way of spiritual martyrdom the hermit enters.

But that is only the beginning of the Way of the Cross, the way of his own death that he has chosen. The other stages of the way bring about the necessity of confronting one's own personality and analyzing oneself in the light of Christ's truth. Realizing how great our weakness, misery, and sin are seems to be the most painful and traumatic experience that a human being can go through. Looking straight at the wound of sin that opens at the bottom of his heart, the hermit experiences the greatest perplexity and pain, but he does not plunge into the abyss of darkness and despair. There is a soothing balm of God's love and grace that enables him to endure those difficult moments with trust and to bear the extreme humility in peace. He gradually comes to see himself in proper perspective, and this is one of the greatest graces a faithful disciple can ever receive from his Lord. This grace comes to him through the severity and simplicity of the desert, through its silence and endless solitude.

The doors of the hermit's heart are closed to melancholy, because it would make his walking on the way of the desert simply impossible. The same does not apply to sadness, as long as it comes from God. Such sadness results from our close relationship with God, in whose brightness the smallest speck of our soul is visible. The sadness goes even deeper – the hermit is sad because of all the sins that offend the majesty of the Lord. Realizing how great is the lack of faith in the world becomes an everyday cross the hermit takes on his shoulders. The Holy Spirit allows his eyes to be filled with tears when he becomes aware of the painful lack of love and faith among Christians. The tears are not merely a sign of human sorrow, but they are a sign of Divine Mercy that allows the hermit to feel and wish what God feels and wishes. They are tears of sorrow, but the hermit is not lamenting himself. What he is lamenting is rather the world, which is indifferent and contemptuous towards the Lord.

The hermit's heart is flooded with tears of grace and filled with unbelievable peace and sweetness. The grace of tears crushes the pride and arrogance that are so deeply rooted in our hearts; it brings us the attitude of tenderness and trust towards God. It also gives us a clear spiritual understanding that enables us to penetrate the depths of the human heart. What comes along with it is the gift of freedom that wants to choose only God and God's will.

If we discover that this clear view of our existential and moral misery is God's gift to us, we will not give ourselves up to despair and depression. Being aware of our insufficiency and weakness, we become spiritually clean and transparent, and we can see, as if automatically, the disposition of our souls. It is not merely a good mental condition reached after a long physical and psychological rest, but it is rather a capability of mind that is achieved through ascetic practices. The transparency of heart that God grants us is the result of Christ's blessing. The hermit can be counted among the blessed, who meet the Lord coming to see them: not yet face to face, but in prayer, the sacraments, and God's Word.

V

THE WAY OF PRAYER

Aperson who goes out to the desert is seeking God. Leaving the humdrum of the cities and finding a place of solitude and silence, the human heart wants to have nothing to hear and nothing to see. Providing such a decision does not result from a psychological disorder, it should in addition be reasonably motivated. In the case of the hermit, the decision is motivated by love. Putting aside all everyday worries, the hermit wants to find a space of freedom where he can talk lovingly and unceasingly with God. Unless solitude is enlivened and sanctified with prayer and contemplation, it becomes a heavy burden, a curse, and a punishment.

1. At the Source of Prayer

The hermit is a man of prayer, a friend of God. The familiar dialogue he holds with God, an intimate conversation that is a loving exchange of two personal freedoms, becomes step by step the real essence of his life. It becomes his daily food and breath, the deepest need of his heart, which leads him into a still new and ever more intensive search. The hermit's prayer is an intense, one-to-one relationship of two persons, a specific game played by two freedoms that reveal to each other the secrets of their hearts. It is impossible for the hermit to turn his prayer into a monologue, meditating on himself or making an unaided trip into the realm of super-consciousness. Every moment of contemplation is for him a conversation of love between the mysteries of two hearts. Every day the hermit turns to God with a cry of love, and God reveals Himself to the hermit in His powerful and all-embracing Word. In fact, the dialogue we hold with God is always our inept response to God's message directed to us in a stream of His Grace. It is the Lord who initiates the meeting, and what is left to us is just to choose to give our humble response of love.

Responding to the gift

Experiencing faith through prayer, the hermit sees the luminous glory of Christ present in the entirety of creation. The world seems to be a transparent veil that covers the Beloved's face. In times of contemplation the Grace of the Holy Spirit allows us for a while to look through the concealing veil and to enjoy realms that surpass anything that we can express.

Every form of Christian prayer can be characterized by dialogue and meeting. The sensitivity we have in faith to inspirations of the Holy Spirit brings about a dynamic spiritual tension between things that are absolute and those that are human. The tension is built up between the reality that is accessible to us in our everyday lives, the reality of our own weakness and limitations, and the ultimate goal of our efforts that is inaccessible to us directly, God. God increases the tension when He gives Himself to us and thus urges us to answer the question that we pose to ourselves. The deepest mystery of human existence remains inaccessible unless we enter the way of prayer that leads us into a new dimension of life. Only then can we truly establish and cement our relationships with God, other people, and the world. So, the gift of Christ's revelation is the crucial moment of Christian prayer. As O'Donnell writes:

> The decisive point then is that God has spoken. God has addressed us and the human person is created by God as dialogical. The human being is created by God to be addressed. Faith is receptivity to this word. This receptivity becomes explicit in the language of prayer. If I know who and what I really am (God's dialogical partner), I will burst spontaneously into the prayer of praise and thanksgiving.[36]

In his search for salvation for himself and for the whole world the hermit faces a mystery, which is the final completion of the universe and time. Only the dialogue of the two freedoms – divine and human – makes it possible for him to fathom the eternal mystery and to unite with it in love. The encounter we mean here is nothing less than an intimate act of engaging the most personal aspects of ourselves. What we are talking about is a contemplative meeting with God to whom we entrust ourselves completely. Though the hermit perceives absolute freedom as present in a secret and mysterious way, it is at the same time present "just-for-him". Prayer as a dialogue and a meeting reveals the truly

---

[36] J. O'Donnell, *The Mystery of the Triune God* (London, 1987), p. 146.

personal character of ourselves, because it makes us able to open ourselves to the Triune Mystery and it puts us "before" and "for" the absolute communion of the Persons.[37]

The dialogue of love

Christian prayer unfolds in a dramatic rhythm of two freedoms – divine and human – that interact with each other through the whole range of mutual relationships and attitudes. God gives us His love through the Spirit and He actively takes care of the world in dramatic action involving the whole of creation, a performance that we can call *Theodrama*.

Therefore, an authentic prayerful dialogue is possible only in the perspective of love. When two persons entrust themselves to each other in love, a wonderful drama of self-giving and co-possessing is played out. The closer the mutual relationships are, the more they determine all the levels of the two partners' personalities. The stronger the ties are, the more silence is needed and, paradoxically, the fuller the mutual understanding is. The knowledge and the fullness of self-giving that spring from prayer are related to the silence of love.

One of the decisive moments in the relationship of love consists in a Paschal "passage". Love takes us from ourselves in order to entrust us to the other person. It is a slow process of giving up, step by step, our own selves, putting aside things that we are acquainted with, that are our own and, as such, are very limited and weak. The Paschal character of love can be clearly seen in prayer, which is a "passage" from what is

---

[37] Cf. T. Węcławski, op. cit., p. 50.

created and limited to eternal life. The one who loves sees his own reflection in the loved one. Love, which shines in prayerful communion, does not strip us of our unique individuality and of the hue of our personal beauty.[38]

Living prayer is a grace of mutual presence and an active disposition of the heart that still longs to be united with the divine "Thou". If prayer is a dialogue in which God originally and solely initiates the relationship, the only attitude the hermit can adopt at the beginning is listening. Only through the attitude of listening can we hear and accept God's voice, touch God's truth, and stop to talk to God. The hermit is not a depositary of the ultimate truth, but he has to keep looking for it in solitude and inner silence. Christ the Word reveals to the human heart still new horizons of grace in order to invite us to live with Him in truth.

> Since we touched Thee, we ourselves have been touched by the breath of eternal life. We cannot find God when we live in the world, nor can we find Him when we leave it. All those who approach the eternal Thou with their entire selves, and who bring the entire self of the world to God, and who also want to offer to God anything that is possible to be offered will find God without any search. God is the *mysterium tremendum* and the highest Thou with whom I want to maintain an eternal relationship. . . . At the same time I am fully aware that my part in this dialogue is to listen and to look. And I need to learn this lesson well, because it will be useful in all my human relationships: to listen and to look is as important

---

[38] Cf. W. Hryniewicz, op. cit., pp. 147ff.

as to speak, for I cannot always make the other listen to me.[39]

Therefore, the hermit's most important disposition, which enables him to lead a life of prayer, is faith. Faith should be seen as being ready, open, and awaiting God's Word that approaches. Living faith shaped by the eremitic experience is not a merely rational effort to accept some more or less clear dogmatic statements on the essence of Christianity. Of course, the role of theological studies seems to be irreplaceable and quite important in eremitic formation. But we need to remember that a true experience of the grace of prayer has to be rooted much deeper than just in the soil of the objective theological knowledge of God and His Revelation.

A prayerful dialogue between the hermit and God can in fact be described as a listening presence in front of a revealing Mystery. The presence looks, listens, and opens itself up humbly and trustfully to the Mystery of the Incarnate God. However, we can ask what the mysterious meeting between the human heart and the unfathomable mystery of God's Word really is. What is the essence of experiencing true faith in prayer, the essence that forms the core of the eremitic life? Where is its deeper meaning to be found, since it cannot be limited to some official statements that we accept or to an outlook on life that we have?[40]

As he progresses on his way of faith, the hermit experiences more and more intimately a new perspective of inner silence, a kind of spiritual space that frightens and amazes him at first because he feels rather lost before it. The

---

[39] J. Bukowski, *Zarys filozofii spotkania* (Cracow, 1987), pp. 125f.
[40] Cf. P. Rostworowski, *Świadectwo Boga* (Cracow, 1996), pp. 43 ff.

experience of faith in the hermit's life must take the form of a radical transition from the world that he knows well and that was the natural soil of his maturation to the realm that is purely spiritual and that an inexperienced traveler may take for a terrible emptiness.

Relational being

In the light of grace the hermit enters into a new quality of being, which is relational being. Faith means our dynamic, intense, and direct relationship with the Father. By meeting God in faith the hermit, guided by grace and truth, is introduced to totally new spiritual horizons. Broad and deep as they are, the new perspectives transcend everything that he has known and experienced so far. Now the rays of Eternal Grace go through and brighten his entire existence, so poor and humble. The Grace radiates so intensely that both its power and its delicate beauty can leave the hermit stunned, lost, or even frightened. Meeting God in faith is not at all a kind of exciting adventure or an interesting hobby we look for in order to have something to boast of. It is rather a difficult, even risky challenge that God presents to us in order to give us a chance of finding and perceiving the invisible presence that fills the space of the human spirit.

Prayer, as the way of finding God whom we have lost because of our sin, often brings suffering into the hermit's life. It also helps him understand more fully the essence of contemplation, which is so important for his spiritual growth. Contemplative prayer begins at the moment when we quit any effort to ponder God and His attributes and decide to enter into a conversation with Him. In other words, the prayerful meeting puts the hermit in a difficult situation when he must allow God to call him "by name", to approach him personally, and to invite him to an intimate conversation. In such a new relationship the hermit feels free from describing God with the word "He" as he used to. Now he enjoys addressing God with the personal "Thou".

An authentic and mature prayer seems to be for the hermit a spiritual perception of faith, a new vision that enables him to recognize God's mystery present at the very foundation of human existence. It is a recognition made in love by one who is loved, chosen, and destined forever to be a child of light. Eventually faith is manifested in prayer as a humble submission of the human spirit, which has become free from any illusions, to the all-embracing reign of the Word, to the Lord's Kingdom.

The hermit as a person of prayer cultivates in his heart the soil where the grace of contemplation can be sown and where it grows. Here we need to adopt an attitude of living in truth, which is an indispensable environment for the Spirit of Truth, the Advocate to come. The *Paraclete* permeates all the levels of human being and brightens up our bodies, hearts, and minds in order to cure and sanctify them. An intense humble prayer in solitude and hiding engages energies that bring us closer in the truth and the Holy Spirit to the Father's face. It would have been impossible for the hermit to search for God, if he had not been originally found and saved by the Lord, and if he did not feel the Lord's merciful eyes fixed on him.

Anointing by the Spirit

The hermit's prayer starts with an explicit and sometimes dramatic pleading for the gift of the Holy Spirit who is, so to speak, the natural environment of Christian contemplation. Any good the hermit receives comes to him along with the grace of prayer. Along with the grace there comes inner joy and peace. The grace of prayer guards him also against the storms of temptation and from physical sufferings. It is a unique balm with which the Father cures the bodies and souls of His closest friends. So many are the paths the Holy Spirit leads the hermit along. Sometimes his heart burns, elevated with great love, and he abides in unspeakable joy, ready to gather all people and the whole world to his bosom. Sometimes, ashamed by his misery and weakness, he humbles himself and counts himself among the greatest sinners. Sometimes again he remains silent and quiet, enjoying the plentitude of spiritual happiness. Those spiritual conditions, diverse as they may be, are lessons of the wise divine pedagogy that leads the hermit to a state of spiritual poverty, inner purity, and faithfulness to the grace received.

The hermit's greatest and never satisfied desire is the grace of unceasing prayer. His longing remains unfulfilled because it aims at things "impossible" by their nature, because it aims at touching and fathoming God Himself. The Christian anchorite is thus always aware that his heart will never be great enough to hold heaven. This is the grace of the Holy Spirit that initiates the urgent desire for prayer, the desire that permeates through the whole existence of the hermit. The human heart, moved by the subtle action of the Spirit, starts to seek the simplest and the surest ways to the Lord.

The very fact of the hermit's thirsting for prayerful communion is a sure sign that he is already embraced by the grace of the Holy Spirit, although he is not fully aware of it. Surprisingly, it turns out that the more we are engaged in an intimate relationship with God, the less we realize that we keep on praying. Thanks to active love, the more our sight is fixed on the merciful Father's face, the more we lose sight of ourselves. Thus, we are not aware of our prayer because we are totally lost in love of the One who has become our life, the meaning of our existence. The practice of prayer reveals the paradoxical logic of true faith, according to which the human heart can enjoy the existential sureness of love, being at the same time completely blinded by the cloud of unknowing. Mature faith does not usually bring about any special knowledge, understanding, or light. It is rather a "radiating darkness" through which we walk to our ultimate destination. For the hermit, the great value and meaning of his prayerful efforts is beyond doubt, but he cannot tell their real direction or course because they are guided only by God.

2. The Practice of Faith

In order to hear the word addressed to his heart, the hermit has to adopt an attitude of faith, which is an attitude of inner openness and silence. Any kind of "noise" – the pressure of thoughts, desires, or words – severely limits our ability to hear and understand. A person of prayer thus tries to achieve silence of the heart, which has nothing in common with spiritual emptiness or an absence of thoughts. Christian prayer can be experienced in the silence of God's presence, a presence that is a gift and that goes beyond time and space.

A method beyond any method

When the hermit wants to pray, he does not do any special "training", nor does he follow any specific procedures such as taking certain body positions, regulating his breath, or purging his mind. His method of prayer is not to have any method at all! He closes the door of his cell and begs God for the gift of the Word and the Spirit that would enable him to perceive in faith the merciful and simple presence of the Father. By being aware of this presence, a free and pure gift, the hermit approaches a broad horizon of inner freedom, so essential for childlike innocence. Anyway, this is the freedom born of the actual experience of faith that makes us able to move along the paths of prayer. O'Donnell writes:

> . . . the Christian's life with the Word is the decisive point which distinguishes Christian prayer from all other types of prayer. This point follows naturally from the unique foundation of Christian experience, namely that God has spoken. Hence God is ever to be found in his Word and this Word can never be bypassed. The danger of bypassing the Word is the danger of all types of mysticism.[41]

In this prayerful dialogue the Divine Word goes out to meet human faith, which is an active response and a submission of heart to a delicate influence of the Lord's glory. On the path of daily prayer the hermit realizes more and more clearly that the capability of seeing the world of God that he gains through faith in Christ is in no way

---

[41] J. O'Donnell, op.cit., pp. 148-149.

natural or a matter of course. On the contrary, it is a miracle of the eternally radiating and shining love of the Father. In recognizing and accepting the miracle of God's revelation, we are greatly surprised and astonished, so we unceasingly desire to know and love God as much as may be possible.

The spaciousness and brightness brought about by the light of the Word protect the hermit from any kind of indifference and from closing his heart to the grace that is still abundantly being given. On the other hand, the gift of the Word allows the hermit to see and to adore the maternal beauty and love of God that has been revealed before the eyes of his heart. In prayer the Christian tries to discern his unique, existential position before God, other people, and the world. In prayer we can understand that we have been created and called by the Father in no other way, but through His Word. Listening to the Word we recognize the gift of God's mercy, the gift of God's fatherly care for us. This recognition makes us feel an intense need of praying the prayer of adoration, which is the fullest expression of our faith. God, through revealing Himself in the Word and through showing His unlimited goodness and glory, gives us the possibility to experience the truth of eternal life, which is the truth about what we have been chosen for, and called to, by God's Word. The gate of our Father's Kingdom has been opened forever in the revealing Word, so the hermit, as a person of faith, considers himself to be the Kingdom's rightful heir.

Unless the hermit falls in love with God's Word, he is not able to comprehend the true meaning of prayer, and he walks the stray paths of nonsense, bitterness, and disappointment. He must take the Word for what it really is, a dynamic reality full of life, which awakens our faith, rescues us, and finally saves us. To meet God is to practice one's faith, the faith born from listening to the Word (Rom 10:17).

Holy reading

Prayer belongs to the order of faith. It is faith that gives the hermit a certainty of God's dwelling in the very center of his humanity. The Holy Scriptures, the living Word, teach us faith in its most original, biblical sense. Faith understood in this way is a mutual relationship of love that binds God and man together, thus it is a relationship that is a covenant. The Bible is the book through which God expresses Himself, wherein He allows His voice to be heard, wherein He reveals His unfathomable mystery and allows us to come to know more about ourselves. To enter the presence of God in the Holy Scripture is to become open to the beauty and grandeur of God's love through a very dynamic and personal relationship. God expresses Himself through the Bible by speaking directly to the heart. The Holy texts are food for the hermit's heart that pines to know and to love God.

The hermit approaches the Holy Scriptures with simplicity and humility, with an openness of faith, trying not to rely only on fruitless erudition that could inhibit his spiritual sensitivity. His usual "method" of reading biblical texts consists in a resilient and frequent return to the verses that caused a profound "movement" of love and understanding in his soul. The anchorites of the early ages used to repeat again and again the biblical verses that for them reflected the whole light of spiritual Revelation. They regaled in the texts' delicate and unique flavor and opened the depths of their soul to the Word that was constantly coming to ignite them anew with love. The reading of the Scriptures provided the hermits with ever-new matter for contemplation. The hermit did not dare to approach the Holy texts unless he first asked the Holy Spirit, whose voice speaks in the Bible, for help – for the light of understanding and wisdom.

The Bible is not a history book for the hermit, neither is it a collection of picturesque and dramatic stories, nor an intellectually challenging source for sociology or philosophy of religion. It remains for him the Holy Book, the source of the truth that he wants to accept and realize and which God allows him to understand. His heart continually needs to be strengthened in faith and purified so that it may be able to perceive the rays of God's light. By being faithful to his chosen way of life, the hermit is ready to deny everything that is not of God and that does not bring a sense of eternity into his soul.

God's word unfailingly leads the hermit on the paths of prayer. No book can be a guide on the ways of contemplation, which are, by nature, simple and ordinary. Contemplation is based on the grace of God's invitation to us to abandon ourselves, to enter into the deepest form of spiritual solitude, to be small and to leave the initiative to God. The only safe way through the spiritual desert is the path of prayer, which leads to enlightenment and communion with God. It is God whom the hermit longs and waits for, living each day in meditation on the Scriptures, which are "the solid food for those who have reached maturity".

3. In the Community of the Church

While discussing the eremitic life, solitude, and silence, we must never lose sight of the fundamental fact that the hermit, like any other Christian, lives in the community that is the Church. There is no doubt that his form of participation in the life of the Church community differentiates him from many other brothers and sisters in faith. However, his whole existence is rooted in the community, and that is the key element that decides the Christian character of the way of the desert.

Reality of the liturgy

Christian prayer is eminently communal in its character. That seems to be obvious, to say the least, due to the fact that it is the Church that provides a proper environment for the bestowal of the Spirit to be really effective. On the one hand, the fact that the hermit is rooted deeply in the community of the Church allows him to achieve the maturity of faith. On the other hand, his active involvement in the life of the Church causes him to desire even more perfect submission and sacrifice for the mission of the Church and to assume a personal responsibility for it.

In fact, the hermit must not cherish the spirit of separation; he must be open to the social aspects of life. He understands perfectly that it is basically the Church as community that rests by the Lord's feet and listens to His voice. The Word, which is addressed to the people, is first accepted and assimilated by the Church, and then it becomes the subject matter of faith for each of Her members. Hence the Hellenistic idea of contemplation, *monos pros monon*,

dating back to the Neoplatonic School, is essentially alien
to the Christian hermit. Therefore the hermit's individual
reception and interpretation of the Word of God is always
rooted in the whole Church's experience of faith. Every form
of worship – individual praise or any other way of venerating
God – gains its power and significance from the fact that it
is really incorporated in the living prayer of God's People,
which is also in the prayer of Christ. Eremitic life is thus
united with the dynamic exchange of gifts that incessantly
takes place in the Church. The hermit who experiences in
faith the reality of the "communion of saints" opens himself
to the exchange of giving and receiving that continuously
goes on in the realm of grace. He is included in the incessant
transmission and reception of the light of God's word that is
actualized also in the sacraments.[42]

For the hermit, as one who listens carefully everyday to
the voice of the Spouse, it becomes necessary and natural to
pass from the deep, silent meditation on the Word to common
liturgical prayer that includes the vocal part as its key element.
Therefore, every authentic effort in the eremitic life has its
special dynamism: it remains in constant relation to the Word
of God that is accessible only in faith and that bears its fullest
fruit in the liturgical community. Being based on and inspired
by the communal reception and experience of the Word,
eremitic contemplation refers to the core of liturgical prayer,
and it seems to be, so to speak, an extension of it.[43]

Thanks to the holy liturgy, the hermit unites himself
directly with the prayer of the Son of God addressed to the

---

[42]   H. U. von Balthasar, *Christian Meditation* (San Francisco, 1989), part III,
chapter 2, "The Way of The Church".

[43]   H. U. von Balthasar, *Prayer*, op. cit., pp. 88ff.

Father in the Holy Spirit. This is both the source and the ultimate fulfillment of the living stream of any authentic Christian prayer. The hermit is deeply convinced in faith that it is exactly the reality of the Church liturgy that by its nature illustrates the dynamism and vitality of the prayer of Christ Himself. Coming in contact with this prayer our hearts become united with the gushing stream of interpersonal Trinitarian love.

The gift of the Holy Spirit given in the liturgy is essentially intended to prepare the community of disciples for their fruitful encounter with Christ. Such preparation primarily aims at forming spiritually sensitive, humble human hearts that are capable of receiving the subtle light of the outpouring of grace. It is the Spirit, the Sanctifier, Who not only reminds us of Christ and reveals Him to the gathered community but also, through His refreshing power, actualizes the redeeming mystery of Christ's Passover.

So liturgical prayer is for the hermit a constant call to spiritual renewal. The hermit, by his constant attempts to renew his faith and love, becomes able to accept the gift of the common prayer of the Church and to strengthen the bonds of love that link him to God and the brethren. The official prayer of the Church surpasses infinitely any individual prayer of each of Christ's disciples. Therefore, the hermit feels moved by the internal impulse of grace, by the urgent call to confess how weak he is when it comes to opening his soul to the mystery of the Passover, the redeeming mystery present in the liturgical celebration. Only such a contrite and humble spirit becomes the fertile soil needed to bring forth the fruit of God's gifts.

The memorial of Christ's Passover

Touching the reality of the liturgy, the hermit touches the mystery of his Lord and Savior. In the center of the liturgy of the Church lies the Mystery of the Eucharist, which is for the hermit a concrete way of realizing his communion with God and the whole creation. This is where Christ consecrates the world and gives perfect glory and praise to the Father. For the hermit, as well as for every other disciple of Christ, the Eucharist is the most precious of all the sacraments, because it is an effective sign of all-embracing and unifying Love.

During the Jewish Passover, Jesus fulfilled His promise made in Capernaum that He would entrust His Body and Blood to the community of His closest disciples. The Priestly Prayer, said during the Last Supper and recorded by St. John the Apostle, constitutes Christ's last will and testament that includes the important call to unity, which is to stem from the Paschal gift of love. The Eucharist, which is the axis of the whole of Christian life, defines the meaning of the eremitic experience as an expression of our constant desire for reaching communion with Christ in trust and faith. Of course the kind of prayerful communion that is present in this sacrament has a universal character. The hermit's prayer leads him to communion with God not only on his own behalf or on behalf of his familiars. Ultimately, this communion is a sacrifice of praise given to the Father, a sacrifice that encompasses the entire history of the universe.

From the very beginning the Church has celebrated the Paschal Supper. In the course of history many liturgical rites have developed, but they all are just different forms of celebrating the same mystery. This state of affairs originates from the mandate that the Lord left us on the night of His Passion: *Do this as a memorial of me.* (1 Cor 11: 24-25) Christ's disciples carry out this instruction by celebrating the *memorial of the Lord's sacrifice.* They offer to the Father all that Christ has offered to them, the gifts of creation: bread and wine, which by the power of the Holy Spirit and by the words of consecration become the Body and the Blood of the Lord.

For the hermit the Eucharistic banquet is, above all, an expression of praise and thanksgiving that we give, together with Christ, to the Father. What the hermit desires fervently is to entrust consciously to God his entire existence, as well as the whole creation, by including them in the sacrifice of Christ. For him Christ's sacrifice is also the best way of giving thanks for every single thing – ultimately good, true, and beautiful – that the Father has done through His Son in order to create and then to save the world. The only sacrifice of praise worthy to be presented to the most high majesty of God can be made solely "through Christ, in Christ, and with Christ," who unites His disciples with His Divine Person, His deeds, and His final glory.

The eremitic life cannot be lasting, mature, or effective until it is marked by a continuous effort to fathom the mystery of Christ's Passover in the light of faith. The hermit should always *remember* the redeeming events of the Paschal Triduum, and the Cross which is their axis. In its significance in Sacred Scripture, a *memorial* is not merely the recollection of past events. It refers to a reality that is much deeper. In it the redeeming work of Christ, given as a gift to the community of disciples, becomes in a certain way present and actual. The Holy Sacrifice of Christ becomes present in the liturgical celebration for the glory of God and for the salvation of the world. The mysterious way in which the salutary events of the Passover are made present is the key to understanding the whole meaning of the liturgy.

Only those who are consciously present to each other can establish a proper relationship of mutual respect and understanding. Our heart cannot trust and enter into a communion with another feeling and loving person until we ourselves are consciously present to him. Nothing else but the heart that is consciously present can entrust itself to and unite itself with another feeling and loving heart. Christ's spiritual presence is made actual in many different ways. The Lord is present in His Word, in the ecclesial community of the disciples, in the poor and prisoners, and finally in the priest who leads the liturgical community. We should remember that this presence is especially pronounced in the celebration of sacred sacramental actions, and most of all in the Eucharist.

The meeting of two loves that are present and open to each other is a necessary condition for prayer to come into existence. It is in contemplative prayer that the hermit touches Christ's presence most intensely. This presence has nothing to do with static persistence. Just the opposite, Christ's presence is ever new, amazingly fresh and full of unknown potential. Through our tranquil abiding in Christ, we can understand better His presence as a gift given to the Father as well as to mankind.

The Eucharist experienced in the context of the eremitic life is also the Paschal banquet of love, a sacred meal shared with the community, a special time when Christ completely gives Himself up to His friends by becoming the food they share. The communal celebration of a banquet is rich in symbolism, yet in its essence it always refers to the sphere of human trust, intimacy, friendship, and finally love. The banquet remains a sign and an expression of the fact that the banqueters come together, that they enter into communion. The Eucharist is not only a meal shared "with the Lord", but it is also banqueting "in the Lord". The community and the communion of the participants possess not only a natural, human character, but above all they are supernatural, divine; Christ takes His seat at the table, and at the same time He Himself is the Supper for His chosen ones.

Meeting Christ and one's brothers at this mysterious Paschal banquet is the greatest mystery of the eremitic life. By virtue of its redeeming character the hermit can find all that he has ever desired, sought for, and expected. Leaning gently and confidently upon the Lord's breast, he experiences intimate union with Him, mutual openness, and dedication. This is what the personal meeting and communion of the Eucharist is all about, and this is what the way of Christian solitude leads us to.

By his participation in the banquet, the hermit deepens his living relationship with Christ. In the Church there is no stronger or more solid foundation for living fully the union of love than receiving the Body of Christ in Holy Communion:

> As I, who have been sent by the living Father,
> myself draw life from the Father, so whoever eats
> me will draw life from me. (Jn 6:57)

As mentioned before, the eremitic life is a way that constantly needs to be animated, purified, and actualized.

The Eucharistic banquet, as a living participation in the Body of the Risen Christ, animated with the Paschal breath of the Spirit, makes it possible to synthesize the two spheres of Christian life that interact with each other, namely, love and faith. The Eucharist shines through and makes up for all the shortcomings and weaknesses that burden our daily lives. It sheds on them the new light of redemption.

The hermit interprets his mission in the most universal dimension. He understands that it is to the world to which God's Word has been addressed, the world to which Christ has been sent. That is why it is so characteristic of and so necessary to the eremitic mission to overcome human limitations by the power of supernatural love. The communal relationship that constitutes the Church has a great influence on the Christian life of solitude.

There are two directions in which the eremitic life, so devoted to prayer, can be oriented. One of them goes "inside" and is an effort of faith that looks closely at the reality of the Triune God in order to deepen our understanding and love for all that refers to eschatological reality. The other extremely different "direction" in the eremitic experience results from the commandment of love for the world. The "outward" direction, which complements the eremitic vocation, is so motivated that it does not pose the threat of distractions or unfaithfulness to the way the hermit has chosen. On the contrary, it is necessary so that the eremitic vocation can be realized. Moreover, the hermit forsakes, so to speak, his individual being, because he wants to follow "Crucified Love" in living for the world. He experiences vividly how the whole universe is included in the drama of Divine Love, the drama revealed in the mystery of the Passover.

4. The Temple of Creation

One of the essential advantages of the eremitic cell is its location amidst the beauty and simplicity of nature. Mysterious woods, an island on a lake, stony plains, or hard-to-reach mountains hold the human heart in awe. The world remains God's temple: a place full of wonders, where He displays His majesty and glory. The cell is a privileged place, where God reveals His beauty through nature, and where a person of faith joyfully learns how to admire and give thanks for it. With his heart open to the polyphonic reality of shapes, sounds, and colors, the hermit tries to perceive and adore the absolute Beauty that shines radiantly through the whole of creation. With the eyes of faith he can pierce through the veil of created beauty and discover the hidden face of his Beloved.

The beauty of nature

The Gospel says that Jesus often used to pray in secluded places – on a mountain or in a desert. His parables are full of images of natural beauty: the lilies of the field, the birds of the air, and the standing grain. The hermits, following Jesus' example, have noticed that meditating on God's Word in a secluded cell and contemplating the world of nature while plowing the fields are closely related to each other. By experiencing directly the beauty of nature, the hermit enters a realm that is purely religious and can more easily attain communion with God in faith.

The hermit knows that it is possible to reach communion with God, who reveals His majesty and His mysterious, elusive presence in nature, in a swift stream, in a quiet, misty valley, in the rolling waterfalls, in the ravishing smell of flowers. Prayer rooted in admiration of the world's natural beauty is an attempt to capture the manifest, but at the same time hidden presence of the eternal Mystery, a Mystery so great that it surpasses all that can be named, measured, or touched. Coming into a close, meditative contact with a mountain, a tree, or a flower, the person of prayer discovers that they all are anchored in a wonderful presence that reaches far above all that we can know through hearing or sight.

In his spiritual voyage the hermit opens his heart to the sense of an unfathomable, mysterious presence – a unique sense of the "sound of silence" that fills the universe. When we look with faith at a picturesque sunset, a white cliff, the greenness of fields, or the grayness of swamps, we can detect the source of every form, which is the eternal presence revealing itself in all visible things. This kind of internal disposition becomes a wonderful, vitalizing prayer of praise and thanksgiving addressed to Christ, the Lord of all things. Though invisible and inaccessible, the presence of God emerges from natural beauty before the eyes of faith and emanates with a new character and a surprisingly new kind of life. The hermit identifies himself with it and thus participates in the all-embracing feast of creation. The orderly form of the world's magnificence enters our minds and hearts and deeply influences our aesthetic and spiritual senses. Such an experience liberates us from the bonds of modern rationalism and breaks the mould of conventions, making our minds and hearts sensitive to every touch of beauty that we encounter.

Such a natural experience, which is close to that of the

biblical authors, poets, and mystics, requires a proper level of spiritual sensitivity. This is the sensitivity that enables us to come into direct contact with the world of nature, the world that shows its mysterious splendor. Our ability to hear the language of trees, to read the poetry of thunder, and to see the good in the world is related also to our living faith that can perceive the unusually rich theological meanings from the open "book of nature". Without the purity and sensitivity that broaden our spiritual horizons, the mystery underlying the universe remains hidden from the eyes of our hearts and our human existence is exposed to the temptation of superficiality.

For the hermit, his spiritual life has its source in a deep trust, a joyful readiness to go out of himself, without any prior reservations, toward the appearing shapes and forms of the world. In other words, his spirituality finds support wherever the favorable environment of freedom appears. Then the world speaks with its own voice and opens before man's eyes its internal sense and logic.

Unconditioned mind

The greatest obstacle in the way of prayer inspired by meeting nature is an enslaved, conditioned mind. Many people on meeting the beauty of the world never notice anything for the simple reason that in fact they are not looking at it at all. This happens because the eyes of their mind are obscured by anxiety, by an attitude of making plans, or by a tendency to focus on the concepts of things, not on real things. The people of the desert incessantly try to get rid of their heart's inclination to feel uneasy and anxious, because all such worries can be a real "cancer" in their spiritual life.

As they listen to the Gospel's call to entrust all our troubles to the heavenly Father, they let go of all their vexations. Having swept away all anxiety and all disorderly thoughts, the hermit's heart falls silent and can now peacefully watch and listen to all that is given to it. The hermit simply learns how to be present before reality, how to persist in total silence and peace, with no concepts, words, desires, or dreams. The hermit "is present to himself" and that is why he can be present to others. In the way of simple meditation, the hermit masters the art of being open and free before the reality of the world and before the Creator.

The prayer of the people of the desert depends to a great extent on their ability to remain internally concentrated and silent, to keep their minds detached from their own judgments, desires, or thoughts. Such an attitude allows them to focus their attention on a particular object, which is the first step on the way of meditation. When we observe nature attentively with an internal fondness, which is love, we allow our minds and hearts to be lifted up to our Creator. Only by achieving such spiritual poverty and wisdom, which is a disposition of being detached from any practical knowledge we have ever acquired, can we face the reality of the world and relate it directly to God.

With his eyes of faith fixed on the world of nature, the hermit can wholly perceive the reality he encounters in the light of truth. Thus, his heart becomes capable of seeing a deeper dimension of existence, and his mind becomes aware of the original holiness of creation. Now the world seems to be for him a special place of God's revelation, God's universal temple. The old Zosima speaks of such a vision:

Love all God's creation, the whole and every grain of sand in it. Love every leaf, every ray of God's light. Love the animals, love the plants, love everything. If you love everything, you will perceive the divine mystery in things. Once you perceive it, you will begin to comprehend it better every day. And you will come at least to love the whole world with an all-embracing love.[44]

Thus, in the eremitic life the mystery of nature is viewed in the context of the mystery of the Christian faith. The hermit gradually discovers the amazing link that connects the reality of God's Kingdom to every single thing and problem under the sun. The world is not only originally and naturally rooted in God, but, moreover, it has been involved in the drama of redemption that climaxed in the Paschal experience. The silence of night, space, the chirping of birds, and the light of dawn are all signs of the vague and secret yet real presence of *Sacrum* in the world. The temple of creation points to a personal presence, which is concealed but at the same time reveals its depths through the clearly written book of nature. The hidden presence is, however, accessible only to a mind that is free from any schemes or habits, and that is ready to meet God's mystery.

The flow of meditation

Direct contact with the world forms in the hermit an attitude of childlike openness and realism that gives him a healthy approach to the reality around him. This attitude is

---

[44] F. Dostoyevsky, *The Brothers Karamazov*, part 2; quoted after W. Hryniewicz, op.cit., p.177.

free from any attempt of imposing his personal desires and expectations on the reality that he is faced with. Everything approached in this way is worthy of respect because of the simple fact that it is unique and created by God. It is impossible for someone who is immature and in search of purely superficial pleasures to be selfless and to look at the world with the eyes of a child, which is why the majority of people feel forced to abandon the way of truth and simplicity in order to live up to others' expectations. This happens because of a lack of prayer and meditation in their everyday lives. The contemporary world often loses its natural sensitivity, its intuitive insight into the reality of creation, and the hermit has a lot to offer it in this respect. By leading people into simple forms of meditation, he can teach them and form in their hearts a sensitivity and respect towards all the forms of life around them.

It seems that the technologically-oriented civilization of today may make it particularly difficult for contemporary people to enter the realm of the *Sacrum*. This is especially true when people, more or less consciously, deprive themselves of their close contact with nature. Yet the hermit goes beyond this. He does not cease praying in the middle of a crowded city or a busy neighborhood, but through faith he is able to feel and perceive God's loving presence everywhere, whether in an airport, a railway station, a supermarket, or the quiet of his cell. All of these places are blessed for him; hence, his ability to fully accept and understand the true value of the world and its people and respect its laws and mechanisms.

Hermits are people who are sensitive and often gifted with artistic talents. While being able to develop their talents, they can also find and appreciate the beauty and the individual characteristics of the heart of the artist hidden in the work. Through his contact with the works of human culture, the hermit finds stimuli to enliven his spirit of esthetic meditation. Any artistic work inspired by wonder and appreciation of the world is, in a sense, a way of participating in the creative energy of God. Indeed, the acknowledgment of the supernatural in all human forms of spiritual culture gives it a much deeper meaning. The hermit is thus able to see the beauty of every work of human hands in the more profound context of God's creative Spirit, not so much due to his sense of esthetic perception as, above all, due to prayer and meditation that are animated by faith.

The contemplative spirit of Christian prayer turns out to be of use in many practical situations of the eremitic life. It helps one, for instance, to adopt a proper attitude towards every field of human culture, such as music, painting, sculpture, and architecture. The hermit excludes nothing that is a reflection of the beauty of God's wisdom from his spiritual life. Ultimately, the encounter with works of human culture turns out to be an encounter with other people as in a fraternal community, which is to some extent an encounter with the original Community of Persons – the Holy Trinity.

The hermit's contemplative prayer, inspired by an esthetic meditation, leads to a greater awareness and constant purification of the spiritual core of his being – his heart. A constantly nourished and renewed faith enables the hermit to "break the seal" of a work of art and see the new, transcendent dimension of reality, and consequently to reach out to the eternal. Pavel Evdokimov illustrates this process by meditation on an icon:

> An icon is never "a window looking out on
> nature" or on any other place, but is rather an
> entire world, "a gate of life" opening before us. .
> . . The result can be truly amazing because when
> looking from our perspective, the various lines
> seem to approach us and give the impression
> that the painted figures are coming out to meet
> us. Indeed, the world of icons is directed towards
> the person himself. Instead of the natural vision
> of our eyes, the vision that makes the lines of
> perspective go into their "point of convergence"
> and makes everything fade away in the distance,
> it offers us the eyes of the heart that see space as
> an infinitely expanding redeemed reality where
> everything is coming out towards a meeting.[45]

It is essential to remember that in the practice of eremitic
prayer, meditation on the beauty of creation is not an aim in
itself. Such esthetic meditation simply prepares the hermit's
heart for receiving the grace of mature contemplation that
is based on simple acts of faith and trust. In order to achieve
inner maturity of spirit, the hermit uses a number of different
and original means, many of which are the result of his own
individual and creative search. This also involves his prayerful
encounter with the world of nature or with the works of
human culture. Each of these elements can be a means of
deepening Christian prayer by influencing our imagination,
spiritual openness, and sensitivity, or finally by forming our
individual sense of beauty. There is no doubt that mature

---

[45] Pavel N. Evdokimov, *La connaissance de Dieu selon la tradition orientale;*
quoted after P. Evdokimov, *Poznanie Boga w tradycji wschodniej* (Cracow,
1996), p.130.

contemplative prayer, characterized by silent perseverance in the darkness of faith, does not require any support in the form of an image or symbol. However, prayer rooted in esthetic experience can have a significant role in the process of reaching such spiritual wisdom.

It is difficult to determine the borderline between esthetic experience and religious life. Today many recognized authors indicate that these dimensions mutually interchange with and determine one another. The hermit is not a refined esthete with a nice taste, whose pride and vanity suffer when encountering things that are less refined and simple. Even though the hermit is often a person with a well-developed sense of beauty, he neither worships it nor considers it a decisive factor in reaching the point of receiving mystical graces. Quite the contrary, the hermit knows that prayer is above all a sphere influenced by gifts of a supernatural nature and not merely a sphere of esthetic sensitivity. Nevertheless, the moment we truly become aware of the presence of God dwelling in the depths of our human self is usually the crowning of our journey of faith which, at the various different stages of its development, was nourished by its encounter with God's Word, nature, and art itself.

5. The Prayer of Existence

The hermit's whole life gradually turns into a single act of love, an act of adoration of God. Every single experience of his is immersed in prayer, so that everything that he says or does is devoted to Christ. A person of prayer feels in his inner being a direct contact with God. Having discovered the uncreated light of the Divine presence dwelling in the temple of his heart, the hermit realizes that his prayer is no longer a matter of mind or heart but rather engages his entire existence. This form of prayer gradually begins to flow like an uninterrupted stream leading to a continuous state of prayer.

At the fount of existence

The hermit, upon venturing into the depths of his heart, comes to the source of his existence, the source that is located outside him in the light of God's presence. He then discovers that his true nature, his deepest identity, is constituted by a loving relationship with the living God, a relationship that reveals itself in prayer. The hermit slowly begins to understand that the whole universe is constantly nourished by a stream of prayer that flows from the hearts of the true friends of God, those that love Him.

Jesus remains the unique model and, at the same time, the source of prayer for the hermit. By His own life and teaching, the Lord gives a wonderful example of perfect harmony between prayer and action, between love for the heavenly Father and love for His brothers. The more intimate the bond that exists between us and Jesus, the stronger and more mature is our relationship with the Father and the Spirit, as well as with every human person. The stream of grace and prayer flowing through one spiritually awakened is brimming with a mercy and gentleness that induce him to mercifully and gently turn to the world. Mature prayer is like a wonderful flower that blossoms with love of neighbor and has a truly divine scent. The hermit ever juxtaposes these two inseparable spheres of Christian life – prayer and ministry to others. The hermit's love takes on the form of mercy and compassion towards the whole of creation. This is what St. Isaac the Syrian wrote on compassionate love:

> What is the compassionate heart? . . . It is the heart that burns for the sake of the whole of creation: the people, the birds, the animals, the demons and all other creatures. When he sees them, he bursts in tears. His compassion and persistence are so great that his heart shrinks, and he cannot bear even the smallest evil or the smallest pain suffered by a created being. That is why in every moment he prays for animals, for the opponents of truth and for all those who hurt him, so that they can be saved and forgiven. The endless compassion that is born at the bottom of his heart, the compassion that is completely open and made in God's own image, makes him pray even for snakes.[46]

At prayer, the hermit comes to realize more and more fully that human life stems from the abyss of the personal, Trinitarian love that exists in eternity. This truth explains and supports his attitude of being rooted in and active in the world. The hermit discovers that every time he leaves God, his infidelity of whatever kind has its source in the sinful rejection of the covenant that was made in faith. Thanks to the grace of faith, God reveals Himself to the hermit as a Gift, a Community of Love. Here we arrive at the very source and essence of Christian prayer. Only the rays of the Presence that reveals Itself as the foundation of all good, truth, and beauty

---

[46] Saint Isaac the Syrian, *Sermons 34 and 81;* quoted after W. Hryniewicz, op. cit., p.177f. See also *Oeuvres spirituelles: Les 86 Discours Ascetiques, Les Lettres* (Paris, 1981), pp. 215, 395.

have the power to awaken the human heart and to lead it towards prayer. For the hermit, to live his existence to the full means to enter into union with the eternal horizon of Triune Love that is present at the core of human existence. It also means allowing oneself to be captured by this transforming, enlightening, and sanctifying infinity.

The prayer of existence experienced by the hermit brings him back to the truth of his existence, to the root meaning of all human action in the world. The existential dimension of prayer provides the hermit with the true meaning of the world's existence. *Since the whole creation is eagerly waiting for God to reveal his sons (Rom 8:19),* a person of prayer, who has the grace of being in a continuous dialogue of faith with the Creator, gives the world its ultimate meaning and participation in the truth of creation and of revelation. Through contemplation, the hermit brings the entire expanse of the universe, together with its particular elements, into the transforming rays of the Passover light. In this way he incorporates the world's claims into the course of redemptive events.

The cloud of unknowing

The beginning of every prayer of the hermit is the confession of his human awkwardness and helplessness (cf. Rom 8:26). This attitude of humility, the attitude of standing in the truth, creates the optimal conditions for the Spirit of all prayer to be imparted. One cannot pray, that is gaze lovingly at the face of God, without the help of the Sanctifier. It is He who teaches us the truth about the Son and the Father. Faith, therefore, as a loving recognition of the truth about the Son, can happen only in the atmosphere of the life-giving breath of the Spirit. The deciding factor behind the efficacy and power of the hermit's prayer is that he beseeches and asks for the gift of the Spirit. In the eremitic life, the Spirit is the One who gives life to the Word and makes it effective. Only the Spirit has the power to truly form the human heart, to make it capable of listening, understanding, and acting in accordance with the Word. The Holy Spirit, Who knows the "depths of God", leads the hermit still deeper into the revealed truth, which ultimately results in his coming closer to the Holy Trinity. Christian prayer is Christocentric, and therefore also "Trinitarian". Christ remains the only way the hermit follows, the way that leads him to encounter the Truth about God. Jesus is also the Gate that leads into the reality of the Kingdom of God, into the fullness of the Holy Trinity.

The dynamism of Christian faith and prayer points to a kind of existential entering into the "cloud of unknowing" that is connected with experiencing the risk of losing one's direction; hence, the special assistance of the Holy Spirit's Grace is absolutely crucial at this point. The *Paraclete*, who illuminates the particular stages of a person's way (His presence was indicated in biblical texts by a column of cloud or a column of fire), leads the hermit through a time of aridity, when he is completely stripped, left only with the Rock, which abounds with nourishing honey. The life-giving light of the Spirit provides him with the strength to overcome his poverty and insufficiency in order to make his way into the unknown. This spiritual exodus, undertaken to find God and inspired with the impulses of grace, can be understood only in the context of experiencing an inner "touch of the Spirit". This is the touch of the Spirit that awakens in the hermit the burning desire to meet Christ that becomes all the more intense and strong the more God tries to satisfy it.

The touch of the Spirit sets the hermit's heart so much on fire that, from that moment on, he cannot rely on anyone or anything except the Lord Himself. Even the relatively rare moments of coming closer to the Bridegroom do not satisfy his desire for communion. Christ usually remains elusive and mysterious, and the rare moments of close intimacy only increase the longing caused by separation.

Experiencing the dialectic of spiritual tensions, the hermit gradually lets go of himself and adopts an attitude of deep veneration and adoration toward God and His will. As his heart expands day by day, he finds in it the source of all life and existence.

The prayerful encounter with the reality of the Holy Trinity, the eternal stream of love and the original beauty, brings delight and inspires adoration stemming from the very center of the Divine mystery. This is the way in which the hermit begins to understand much better that the mystery of his own existence, as well as the Mystery of the universe, is originally rooted in the revelation of merciful Love. Being spiritually awakened to live by pure faith and love is one of the most precious gifts of grace that the hermit is offered in prayer.

Whether or not we enter the way of mature prayer is to a large extent dependent on whether or not we recognize the love that the Father has for us in Christ. Authentic spiritual life does not depend on any prior assumptions, plans, or ideas. It always results from the Lord giving Himself to us in abundance, so effectively as to bring us to spiritual conversion and enlightenment. Spiritual life is essentially such a complete openness of the human spirit that it gives a lasting sense of the Lord's presence, which can be experienced in every moment of our everyday lives. No form of deeper contemplative or mystical experience can occur without this prerequisite grace that leads to the way of prayer. Openness of heart is particularly reflected by the hermit's increasing desire to imitate Christ in His Paschal experience. So who is Christ in the eremitic experience of prayer, and what role and place does He have in opening our hearts?

In relation to suffering

The Christian religion draws its vitality from Christ's Incarnation, which is why the reality of the Word Incarnate is the foundation of spiritual growth and maturity stemming from an attitude of submission to grace. It might seem that the grace of the eremitic vocation should have cut a person off from any form of communal life and from the problems of this world. But the many examples of great hermits reveal that any authentic spiritual experience, which in its very nature is a culmination of love, leads to an attitude of ministry. Catholic mysticism has never meant contemplating one's own self. On the contrary, the dynamic way of the imitation of Christ has always been both a characteristic and a deciding factor of Catholic mysticism, and without it no spiritual development can occur. What is more, this "imitation" particularly concerns the events of Christ's Passion, because the ability to endure suffering remains a sound measure of the authenticity of one's commitment.

Eremitic prayer, which is both dynamic and rooted in the supernatural potential of love, treats the gift of suffering and the sacrifice entailed in it not only as a source of constant vitality and renewal, but also as a means of protection from pride. Suffering clearly illustrates the basic characteristic of love, namely, the act of entrustment of oneself to another person. It is hard to imagine how we can entrust ourselves to a person we love without taking the risk of being torn apart and painfully wounded. C.S. Lewis' words are worth quoting in this regard:

> To love at all is to be vulnerable. Love anything, and your heart will certainly be wrung and possibly be broken. If you want to make sure of keeping it intact, you must give your heart to no one, not even to an animal. Wrap it carefully round with hobbies and little luxuries; avoid all entanglements; lock it up safe in the casket or coffin of your selfishness. But in that casket – safe, dark, motionless, airless – it will change. It will not be broken; it will become unbreakable, impenetrable, irredeemable. The alternative to tragedy, or at least to the risk of tragedy, is damnation. The only place outside Heaven where you can be perfectly safe from all the dangers and perturbations of love is Hell.[47]

Suffering endured in the spirit of faith and prayer frees the hermit from selfish inclinations and enables him to undergo a spiritual rebirth. Uniting prayerfully the pain of our own existence with the suffering of Christ, incorporating our own existential wounds into His Cross, is the only way we can fully and unconditionally offer ourselves to Christ. When going through a time of suffering and during all other

---

[47] C.S. Lewis, *The Four Loves* (Glasgow, 1963), chapter VI, "Charity".

dramatic moments of life, it seems we are left on our own in the darkness of our existence, emptiness, and nakedness. The only light we can hope for is the light shining from the Cross, the instrument of our redemption, where divinity and humanity meet.

The ability to take up the prayer of suffering is a sign of the hermit's spiritual maturity. Our prayer of suffering refers essentially not to our own personal sufferings, but also to those of the whole world, both references being an integral part of our prayer of petition. The existential prayer of suffering entails a very conscious effort to imitate the Savior and an acceptance of every humiliation and disgrace possible.

Together with Christ, the hermit shows his solidarity with the suffering sinner and wants to take part in the drama of God's love, even to the point of going down into the abyss. The symbol of the Cross always remains the sign that confirms the credibility of the hermit's mission and presence (Mt 16:24-25). The mystery of the Cross paradoxically reveals the truth of Christ's words in saying that His yoke is easy and His burden light. It is through the Cross of the Lord that the hermit receives the grace of participating in the unfathomable mystery that enables him to understand the ultimate meaning of life and death.

The *via regia*, the royal way of suffering, unveils its mystery only before a person capable of receiving God's gift of wisdom. Without being anointed with the oil of the Holy Spirit, without reaching mystical union through the reality of the Cross, one cannot break through the mysterious darkness of suffering. Taking up this most difficult form of prayer in earnest, the hermit brings elements of light, love, and peace into the world that is so very thirsty for them. These are the first fruits of the Kingdom of God, which bring joy, peace, and spiritual enlightenment. This Kingdom is the Kingdom of the freedom of the children of God, who look up to the eternal mystery.

6. The Prayer of Mary

The hermit, who learns how to pray in the school of Jesus, is at the same time a disciple of Mary, His Mother. She truly is Queen of hermits; it is she to whom God said that He would lead her out into the wilderness and speak to her heart (cf. Hos 2:14). Mary's faith was so pure and so very open to the reality of the Word of God that no other faith was as pure as hers, which is why the Word came to live in Mary not only in a spiritual sense, but also physically. She conceived in prayerful solitude and silence of heart and thus remains the Mother of Christian prayer. This means that her perfect union with the Word gave her the power to guide her brethren along the way of the mature life of prayer. Her Son, Jesus Christ, is the Way that leads us to the Father in the Holy Spirit and the Way that she wants each of the faithful to follow.

The sanctuary of the Spirit

The hermit looks to Mary as the most perfect work of the Holy Spirit's mission. The *Paraclete* encompasses all the aspects of her life and brought the Virgin's faith, hope, and charity to their perfection. Even before the Incarnation of the Word, Mary meditated and prayerfully contemplated the reality of God in the simplicity of faith. Her life and everything she went through was formed by her urgent need of listening, meditating, and contemplating God.

Mary is the one who illustrates the essence of the eremitic lifestyle in the simplest and clearest way. She is the unique and unmatched synthesis of Christian perfection, the model that every hermit would like to realize in his own life. Thus the hermit lets Mary come into his life and has a filial relationship with her.

Strange though it may seem, the hermit does not build his life on a sense of autonomy and independence. As he gradually frees himself from his attachment to himself and to worldly things, he offers God his freedom, thoughts, and deeds, just as Mary did.

The Blessed Virgin Mary's prayer is completely focused on eternity. Mary's contemplation, stemming from the mystery of the Incarnation, is a support for the hermit in every stage of his meeting with God. The Annunciation, and the pouring out of the Holy Spirit that occurred then, was so unique that it bore the fruit of God's dwelling in time. We should therefore be oriented towards Mary as the archetype of the eremitic experience of prayer. Her mystical experience reveals the mystery of the communion between God and man. From the very moment of the Annunciation, through the darkness of Calvary, up to the glorious light of the Easter morning, her heart was engaged in a loving adoration of her Son.

The three fundamental attitudes that a hermit in Mary's school of prayer wants to adopt are: conscious presence (*Ecce*), the obedience of faith (*Fiat*), and the prayer of glory (*Magnificat*).[48] The hermit's meeting with Mary, along with the fruit it bears, is one of the most precious gifts of the Holy

---

[48] Cf. L. Chenevière, *Rozmowy o milczeniu* (Cracow, 1984), p.177; also *The Hermitage Within* (Cistercian Publications, 1999).

Spirit that he can receive in his life. He meets the Mother and, following the example of St. John, he makes a place for her in his home. To make a place for Mary in one's home means to offer her one's body, heart, and spirit, one's whole self, so that all prayer and action start to flow through her and in her. Thus, to offer ourselves to Mary is to solemnly accept the will of the Father (*Fiat*) to the very end.

Prayer in the school of Mary refers to an ever-greater entrustment of ourselves to God and to the unconditional offering up of our freedom to Him. We are not, however, able to do this unaided, which is why the hermit calls upon Mary with the words of St. Bernard:

> Remember, O most gracious Virgin Mary,
> That never was it known
> That anyone who fled to thy protection,
> Implored thy help or sought thy intercession,
> Was left unaided.

The *Magnificat* is the sacrifice of praise that the hermit offers together with Mary. The prayerful atmosphere of his cell is, above all, an atmosphere of joy and spiritual peace. The hermit, entrusting himself with Mary to God the Father, is granted the "spirit of wisdom" that guides him through the inscrutable paths of mystical contemplation. It is in Mary's heart that he finds the gift of supernatural wisdom, because it is her contemplation that draws the fullness of the Holy Spirit's presence. It is a fullness that meets the unique personal perfection of Mary. Experiencing this abundance of gifts – which in reality come down to one Gift, the gift of the Son – she never concentrated on herself, but rather abandoned her own self out of love for God and neighbor.

As she listened in prayerful meditation to the word of God, Mary opened her womb to the Giver of life and passed Him on to the whole of creation in the mystery of the Passover. The Mother of God is called the "Seat of Wisdom" not only because it was in her womb that Eternal Wisdom became flesh and revealed Himself to humanity, but also because she is the "chosen place", that is overshadowed and nurtured by the Spirit of all wisdom and fertility. The hermit can therefore hear her motherly call, echoed in the Scriptures, directed to him:

> Come to me, all you that yearn for me,
> and be filled with my fruits;
> You will remember me as sweeter than honey,
> better to have than the honeycomb.
>
> He who eats of me will hunger still,
> he who drinks of me will thirst for more;
> He who obeys me will not be put to shame,
> he who serves me will never fail.
>
> (Sir 24:18-21)

The Rosary

The hermit's spirituality is formed under Mary's maternal care. She herself guides his prayer, since the Most Blessed Virgin Mary does not obscure anything, but is always present wherever the meeting between God and man takes place. Just like the column of fire in the Exodus, she becomes the unique horizon for the meeting and dialogue between God and mankind. Thus, the hermit who finds God in Mary discovers Mary as the chosen portion of the great community of the saints of God. By joining the Virgin Mary's prayerful circle, the hermit immerses himself in the atmosphere of the Holy Trinity as though immersing himself in the climate of all those that are already saved.

The rosary is the way by which the hermit meets Mary. This prayer enables him to meditate with Mary on all the events of the Gospel. The whole eremitic tradition confirms the unique role of this form of Christian prayer, as the rosary is a time of silence, a time of listening and gazing with Mary at the revealed truth. The simplicity of the rosary brings together vocal and meditative prayer and allows us not only to focus our loving attention on God, but also to become a part of Mary's prayer, of her silence, obedience, and devotion to God. In this way Mary herself, or rather the Spirit of the Father, prays in the hermit. This is probably the key to the amazing power and efficacy of this prayer.

By praying the rosary, the hermit descends into himself and, thanks to the grace of the Holy Spirit, comes to know himself better and accepts the mystery of his life that essentially is related to the mystery of the Triune God. Thus, rosary meditation makes it possible for us to find, awaken, and constantly purify the source of our personal subjectivity, which is our heart. The heart, in the biblical sense of the word, is the foundation of our human personality, the core of our "self", where we truly remain ourselves. The human heart is the dwelling place of God, of His Word and His Spirit. The simple prayer that he offers up together with Mary allows the hermit to solve, in the most natural, spontaneous, and beautiful way, all of his urgent existential problems.

Mary is a true help to the hermit in discovering his own identity, vocation, and mission ever more fully. In other words, the special gifts of the Holy Spirit bestowed on Mary enable her to intercede for the hermit so that he can obtain the grace of discovering the true name that the Father has given him. With such powerful intercession it is hardly surprising that even the Desert Fathers had given her the title of *Omnipotentia supplex* [Suppliant Omnipotence].

The Christian hermit is someone who has a great love for the Mother of God. This love is a very great charism that he has received from the Father. Mary is always with him, and he is deeply aware of this exceptional gift. Through her mystical presence, particularly during prayer, the hermit can almost "see" Mary with the eyes of his heart and entrusts all his personal problems and those of the whole world to her.

7. Towards Contemplation

The hermit strives for the most simple and most direct contact with God in his spiritual life. The eremitic tradition illustrates the fundamental aspect of eremitic spirituality of experiencing faith and the Divine Mystery in a profound and peaceful way. As his faith matures, the hermit begins to experience and perceive the presence of God ever more clearly in his life. It is possible for him to experience God's presence in the peace and quiet of his life, which make up the natural environment of his faith.

Receiving mercy

The encounter with God's Word in meditation, together with an openness of mind to the glory of God revealed in nature and in the works of human culture, leads us to a way of expressing admiration and praise to Christ, who shows His Father's magnificence. Contemplation leads us to fix our eyes on God's eternal glory. God's love that is revealed in the world becomes so visible to the hermit that it becomes his only motivation and fulfillment in following the way of the desert. Contemplation forms a specific structure of faith. It deepens the hermit's faith because it leads to a better understanding of God, the world, and himself. The glory of God's love, tenderness, and mercy requires us to keep our hearts open. The face of God, who stoops down to our human poverty and weakness, should be the object of contemplation.

The reliability of the love that is absolute allows one to adopt an attitude of trust and openness towards God's wonderful revelation. Simple forms of contemplation, based on encountering the Word of God and on the liturgy, are a unique source of inspiration. The experience of contemplation leads to an ever-stronger feeling of God's presence, a feeling expressed in acts of praise and adoration.

As he looks for God on the paths of contemplation, the hermit often experiences his own weakness. In the shining light of God's mystery, his efforts of fathoming God prove to be futile. In contemplation, God reveals His unique face, yet the hardships of the earthly journey intensify the longing for the ultimate goal of all human efforts. Focusing all one's desires and attention on God is a characteristic of the search for God on the way of contemplation.

When the whole spiritual search becomes concentrated on the one simple desire of wholeheartedly adhering to Christ, the hermit's contemplation turns into an attitude of trustful perseverance before the Father. The intense longing to gain a better understanding and greater love of God can take on many different forms. God initiates a drama of love in which He sometimes seems to be hiding behind a veil of omnipotence and inaccessibility, and sometimes reveals Himself, and at the same time pulls us towards Him.

The contemplative experience of faith often turns out to be a meeting with emptiness, a meeting that brings about a kind of anxiety stemming from the ever-new horizons arising before our eyes. This situation is a sign of the hermit's helplessness and inner weakness. He comes to realize more and more clearly that his only chance is the hope that God reveals His face and looks upon him with mercy. Christian contemplation opens the eyes of our hearts to the unfathomable reality of the Spirit, which is why the spiritual knowledge stemming from contemplation remains incomplete and vague, yet at the same time gives a confidence of faith.

The spiritual rock

Since the contemplative perception of the truth is based on the grace of faith, the hermit should abandon all that is not God in order to start a new life established on the confidence of faith. Christ should remain the only "Rock" on which he builds his life. Contemplation cannot be generated by our systematic efforts or by specific techniques but is rather the result of the presence of the theological virtues, that are both something we strive for and something we receive. Eremitic contemplation is both a dialogue of faith conducted in the Spirit and a reality of love, a unique relationship between God and man.

The way of our Lord Jesus Christ is the only way the hermit follows, for it is through Christ that we come to know the Father. The Paschal way of Christ is the only way of finding God in the desert. Therefore, all the hermit's spiritual efforts come together into one in the mystery of contemplative prayer. The discovery of God through contemplative prayer can lead to a transformation of our human existence into a life full of light and peace.

Contemplative prayer encompasses the whole of the spiritual life and aims at the reception of the Gifts of the Holy Spirit, especially the gift of wisdom. That is why the hermit, wanting his faith to become mature, must at a certain stage of his spiritual journey start to pray the prayer of contemplation, which is a true crowning of his intense spiritual effort. Contemplative prayer expresses, and at the same time intensifies, the virtues of Christian faith and charity, by which the hermit can become a true disciple and friend of Christ. In contemplative prayer, a person can start to appreciate through faith how great and unfathomable God's mystery is and how much it surpasses all human attempts of understanding it.

The decision to undertake the eremitic life and contemplative prayer is therefore very much related to a change in the way we perceive and treat ourselves, the whole of creation, and God. And this depends on how much we allow the loving hand of God to lead us and take hold of our lives. It is up to us to recognize and remove any obstacles standing between God and us, so that He can give His love freely to us. Our spiritual endeavor at contemplation is necessary so as to get rid of all the things that are obscuring God's action in our lives, which will allow us to notice and appreciate that action all the more. The growing awareness of the Father's loving presence makes it easier for us to reach full communion with Him. The spiritual peace that we receive allows us to abandon all forms of unnecessary activism. The moment we submit to the intensive action of the Holy Spirit, we will experience the greatest and most profound joy at being unconditionally loved.

VI

THE WAY OF SERVICE

We go to the desert in search of mercy, meekness, and simplicity. There is no place here for any artfulness, diplomacy, or pretence. By giving up all his habits and the like, the hermit wants to enter a new reality and experience a different dimension of time and space. His heart yearns for what is eternal. The desert makes it possible for him to leave the world of the profane and invites him to a new order of things that are unfathomable and intangible.

1. Towards a New Quality of Existence

The absolute glory of God that is revealed in the hermit's life urges him to adopt a new characteristic of existence, a quality rooted in simplicity and truth. The hermit is thus called to continual conversion and to rebuffing all temptations of insincerity, hypocrisy, and lies regarding himself and the world. His living faith encourages him to devote himself to a ministry where sorrow, suffering, hope, and joy constantly interchange with each other. The hermit is a person who strives to make truth and goodness present in his life. To become a mature human being means to leave behind what is false in order for the full beauty of our Christian calling and mission to be revealed.

Values in crisis

The complex situation of contemporary culture and civilization calls for reevaluation and change. A distinctive trait of modern times is that all human values are perceived only on the horizontal level, in a secular and purely human way. Human dignity, solidarity, and brotherhood are no longer seen in the context of religious experience and in relation to God, but solely as the achievements of secular culture.

The sincere and authentic attempts contemporary people make to propagate equity, justice, brotherhood, and peace are undoubtedly an expression of the noblest and most creative powers of the human spirit, which overcomes its own limitations in acts of service and sacrifice. However, seeing man and his actions as the only source of all values is radically and dangerously limiting for the understanding of values. We should, therefore, put the achievements of human hearts and minds in a broader context: in relation to that which is absolute.

The faith and the way of life of the hermit make him naturally open towards all that is universal in the human culture. In undertaking this way of life, the hermit wants to receive the light of grace, because he realizes how weak, limited, and miserable he is before the fullness of Christ's glory. Only through maintaining our close relationship with Christ, which is a relationship of faith, are we are able to restore our true selves and our own true identity. Is not the ultimate sense of salvation to tie a thread of reconciliation between God and man, between man and the world?

In this universal reconciliation we, as individuals, find our true and mysterious names by which God calls us, one by one, to Himself. Salvation encompasses the entire human being, including the realm of human values. The hermit knows well that both human existence and the system of human values should have their own manner of existence and should serve one another. This is possible only when both the human being and human values are redeemed, that is, directed towards salvation and put in the perspective that restores original relations. Therefore, the world of culture and its values should also be redeemed and opened up, so that God's splendor may shed light on them and illuminate them.

Eremitic ethos

The universality of the eremitic vocation is manifested in the fact that it not only encompasses and transforms the person in question, but also affects much broader circles. The extent of its influence is closely related to the redemptive power of Christ's mission, as it is this power that should be made manifest in this vocation. This cannot occur unless the hermit lives in the spirit of humility and service, and unless the redemptive power of love transforms him and makes him capable of self-giving and sacrifice. The authenticity of the hermit's way should be expressed in transparency in relation to the truth and beauty that are revealed here. The greater the interior freedom of the hermit and the closer he comes to the truth of his existence and himself, the more he can enhance the values present in his life and in the history of the world.

The fundamental value in the hermit's life is the relationship of friendship between himself and God. In order for this friendship to be cultivated and developed, it calls for fidelity even to the point of sacrifice. This sacrifice is based on entrusting ourselves to God and not depending solely on our own knowledge and judgment in making decisions in daily life. This decision of submitting our human freedom to eternal love often causes us pain and perplexity. It turns out that the dynamism of the growth of Christian faith has a bipolar structure that goes from light to darkness, from glory to humiliation. We know from the experience of many spiritually deep and mature people that the growth of faith, as well as the process of opening up to higher values, leads through many painful and difficult experiences in life. Things that are beautiful and eternal can only be realized through love, sacrifice, and service. This is what the way of the desert really signifies.

The hermits discover a new dimension of existence, which is fully permeated with the light of the resurrection, by abandoning themselves and adopting the attitude of a servant. The hope of life despite death becomes the source of energy necessary to search for truth and goodness in life. In light of the resurrection, redemptive love saves all that is valuable and beautiful and puts it in the perspective of eternity.

The capacity of discovering and realizing the principal human values in the hermit's life naturally affects the whole domain of freedom. The essential point here is to adhere to the truth of one's own existence in concrete, everyday decisions. Standing untiringly by truth and love is a concrete expression of sacrificing one's life for them. The personal growth of the hermit is only possible in serving those values, accepting and realizing them in his personal vocation. Moreover, serving these values also means directing others towards them, thus confirming their objective presence.

A love that is open toward all possible good gives us the chance to decipher the most original ontological revelation present in creation. The discovery that every creature is good and beautiful is the decisive point in the process of accepting Christ's message, with its radical simplicity and depth. When we consciously and faithfully devote ourselves to strengthen the truth, goodness, and beauty in this world, there comes a moment where earth unites with heaven, nature with grace, and things that are human with those of God.

In praise of humanism

Is not the life of the desert a paean of praise for a certain form of humanism? Is not the very fact of posing such a question a provocation?[49] The possibility of discovering one's own identity is one of the most important fruits of living a life of solitude and silence. This gift of coming to know one's human identity is part of a greater gift of being introduced into the mystery of Christ and His Passion. Therefore, Christians can realize their humanity evermore fully upon entering the realm of spiritual solitude. It is difficult to define the process of this personalization, because it applies to all the levels of human existence and is consequently endless. This process has no end, because at every stage of one's personal growth there is always a part of our personality that has been left out and has not yet been put into the light of Christ's truth.

The hermit cannot progress on the paths of faith unless

---

[49] Cf. T. Merton, *Life and Holiness,* op.cit., pp.130f.

he makes every effort to develop his own humanity. Being a Christian means being human in the most profound sense of the word. It also means the conscious effort to realize God's image in oneself throughout one's life. The Christian hermit can in this sense be considered a humanist and his path a way of strengthening justice, equity, and brotherhood in the world. The eremitic vocation, therefore, protects and fosters the dignity of every human being.

The eremitic ethos is based on the principle of primacy, of putting in first place that which is creative, right, wise, good, and beautiful. The hermit can accept any form of humanism that serves the human good. Every route that leads to the mystery of the human being also leads to the mystery of God. Although this process is often vague and hidden, the truth of the Gospel leaves no doubt about it. The human face is one of the most privileged "places" where God's image is revealed. There have been many humanistic trends and orientations in the history of human thought. Some of them – like classical, renaissance, or existential humanism – brought new hopes for a better world, but were very fleeting and soon led to disappointment. The modern trends of secular humanism, with their revolutionary or technological orientations, are likewise going through a crisis today.

The humanistic orientation of the eremitic life relates to the absolute and the eternal. The faith we have in Christ allows us to overcome any shadow of doubt concerning our salvation. The hermit is not an ideologist who attracts others with a utopian vision of the new humanity. He will not support projects, plans, or structures that want to "accommodate" us to the worldly order of financial gain and self-interest, because the life of faith is not a mere pragmatic philosophy of living. The hermit is indeed a true friend of humanity, and his love for humanity is not invasive but reveals a true freedom and sincerity of heart. The gift of friendship is a shelter and a delicate care offered to another person. It breaks all the barriers of perplexity and fear.

Many different terms have been used in trying to define the most fundamental dimensions of human existence and determine the value of the human being. A lot of time and effort has been wasted in order to find the proper definition of man: *Homo sapiens, Homo ludens, Homo faber, Homo creator.* All these try to determine the most important elements of human existence. Many schools of humanism and anthropology have tried to fathom the mystery of the human being, but true human nature still escapes their understanding. The mystery of human existence will remain unfathomable as long as we approach it as something static and separated from the reality of life. To understand the human person is to approach and gain an insight into the mystery of love and the mystery of all the relations caused by love. The mystery of human nature is revealed in the One who gives testimony to unconditional love by giving up Himself for the salvation of the world.

2. The "Sacrament" of Friendship

It turns out that the desire to find the ultimate meaning of human existence, that is, God Himself, cannot be satisfied without undertaking very concrete acts of asceticism. In fact, the eremitic way of life is marked with the bloodstained footprints of Christ. The hermit follows in his Lord's footsteps up to the mountain peak, which is concealed by the dark clouds of terror and the light of glory. This is where the conscious decision to follow the way of poverty, obedience, and humility, up to the point of the ultimate humiliation of the Cross, takes place. The hermit's inner simplicity and spirit of asceticism are expressed by his fervent desire to give up everything, including his own "self", out of his love for Christ.

Tempted by heroism

It is not that difficult to settle down in a hermitage. It remains a possibility for almost anyone. We often meet heroic people who are ready for many sacrifices in today's world. They may live in barracks, have little sleep, work hard for long hours day and night, and live on bread alone. Therefore, it would seem that those are many who would make good hermits. But is this really the case?

Only a person who knows nothing about the question could give a positive answer to this. The mere decision to take on this way of life or to attempt heroic deeds is not the central core of the eremitic life. The art of being a hermit consists in the ability to undertake peacefully all the daily chores of the solitary life not for one year or ten, but for one's whole life. We cannot say that we have chosen to follow the eremitic vocation unless we are truly rooted in the desert of silence and prayer that become a necessity for us. If a hermit attempts to be "heroic" and successful, if he tries to make the world admire his efforts, he is greatly mistaken about the essence of his vocation.

It is simplicity, trust, faithfulness, and an authentic lifestyle that make the vocation what it truly is. The eremitic experience consists in a countless number of simple daily occupations that are undertaken in a contemplative and joyful spirit. Every day consists of prayer, meditation, cleaning, preparing meals, receiving guests, taking a walk, and chopping firewood. It combines the joy of a feast with the solemnity of fasting, the gift of friendship with the readiness for forgiving all enemies.

The hermit's life cannot be creative unless he gives up all attempts to perform extraordinary and spectacular deeds and unless he becomes like a little child, who welcomes each day with joy and lightheartedly bids farewell to it at sunset. In other words, the hermit can become his true self as soon as he understands that his greatness is in the humble acceptance of his weakness, his human condition, and of the earth that carries him so patiently. His true greatness and radiating beauty are rooted in his gratefulness to God for every single day of his life, for the love that he experiences, and for the gift of his body that makes all the gestures that are a sacrament of that love possible. The hermit becomes himself only when he serves.

The gift of presence

Everybody needs a friend, somebody we can share our problems with, who will bring the light of hope and safety into the dark and difficult days of our life. A friend is a person who provides us with the shelter of love and who brings us the gift of peace and tenderness. The hermit is called to be the friend of every one of his brothers and sisters. Since he himself feels deeply loved and accepted by the Love that is eternal, his desire is to share that goodness and peace with others. The gift of friendship that he offers is, above all, a gift of his peaceful ability to listen to and accept every human problem, heartache, and even despair. He must be wise and brave in order not to get frightened by the human misery and loss he sees. The other person then draws a sense of stability and calm from his inner balance and peace.

When he listens with a love and silence to all the troubles and secrets that others entrust to him, he does not want to judge, evaluate, or condemn them. On the contrary, he lets their words flow, so that they can be freed from any anger, fear, or sorrow and so be transformed into a natural and spontaneous joy. The only thing that is really needed here is a simple presence of love that brings warmth and peace to the deepest levels of the human personality.

Friendship plays an important role in the hermit's life, namely that of witness. God manifests His presence in the world through the very sign of friendship and thus invites people to a meeting and to dialogue with Him. A friend is "a sacrament" of God Himself, a gift and a grace given so that the other person can be delivered and saved. A friend, through his loving, accepting, and warm presence, reveals the merciful and caring face of God. Human pain and distress, therefore, are a call to give up our "hearts" to others, to give them the best and most beautiful part of us.

Selfless friendship and love in this manner become a way of realizing the deepest meaning of being human, a meeting-place of things human and things divine. One of the best instruments of evangelization the hermit has is his friendship and his simple love for his brothers and sisters. No one can witness to the truth of the Gospel without giving his life to others. The hermit has to be a servant to all those in need in order to keep his friendship selfless. Just like a child's smile, the smile of friendship expresses an inner openness and trust able to transform hearts, give new energy in life, and thus become the straightest way to unity and freedom.

A fellow traveler

The hermit tries to be a friend to all, but especially to those who turn to him looking for advice and support. The presence of the hermit, familiar with the ways of God's wisdom, seems to be helpful and even indispensable to those seeking light on the ways of prayer. The hermit, humbly reluctant to undertake such a task, makes a good "traveling companion" on the ways of prayer. If he ever assumes the role of such a spiritual companion, he patiently and faithfully points out to all the obstacles standing in the way of reaching full communion with God in prayer.

Taking on the role of a spiritual companion on the paths of prayer, the hermit is fully aware of his task as being a service of love to help others adopt an attitude of openness towards approaching God. This great charism that he has been given as part of his vocation enables him to rekindle the tiny spark of God's life in others. This is usually a very difficult task, and there are many different factors that determine its success. Of course, a fundamental factor is that the hermit actually has the charism to undertake this.

It goes without saying that, in today's difficult times and cultural crisis, the hermit certainly should take on the role of a guide who helps others find their way back to prayer. By consciously taking on the task of opening up the unfathomable treasures of Divine Mercy to others, the hermit undertakes a very delicate, complex, and highly responsible mission, a mission of service to every one of his brothers and sisters. Everybody looking for new inspiration in the

Christian life can count on the hermit's advice and spiritual support.

The hermit desires neither to be a master nor a teacher of others. His life should, however, remain a clear and distinct sign of God's presence to all who look to him. This mission comes to an end when a person under his guidance finds himself under a very direct action of grace and enters into intimate communion with God. A spiritually mature hermit is naturally a very gentle and discreet person, capable of displaying great empathy for those who seek his support. On the other hand, his spiritual sensitivity and thoughtfulness make him capable of recognizing the very moment when his mission as a spiritual director comes to an end.

The hermit is too wise to yield to the temptation of taking the place of God. The Gift of the Spirit that he has been given enables him to transmit the rays of God's glory to those who await them and, as a true friend of God and man, the hermit humbly tries to step aside after he shows others the best ways of entering into and deepening their personal relationship with Christ. Indeed, he cannot be a good spiritual companion on the paths of prayer unless his love becomes "transparent" to the Mystery that is being revealed. Of course, the effectiveness of his spiritual advice is dependent on the extent that he himself recognizes and understands God's presence in his own life. It is only through his mature faith that the hermit can successfully accompany others on the ways leading to full communion with God.

It is essential that the hermit have, apart from his practical experience of faith, the gift of wisdom and a sound theological knowledge of the spiritual life. These elements are crucial and enable him to find the best approach to leading uniquely every individual according to his specific situation.

The way of the desert is full of paradoxes. The hermit dwells in solitude in order to truly meet God and other people; he remains silent so that his words are wise and accompanied by God's grace; and he fasts in order to learn how to celebrate with true joy. Perhaps these apparent paradoxes of his life make it easier for him to accept the paradoxical situation of being a spiritual director, because he must be fully aware that he has been called to give what of himself he cannot give: to constantly point to the realm that remains beyond any possibility of human perception, and to lead others onto the paths of God, that have no beginning and no end.

Though the hermit helps other people through his charism, he cannot relieve them of their personal responsibility for their spiritual growth. The mature spiritual companion knows well that, on his own, he can give nothing to those whom he assists. But above all, he does not want to force anybody to choose the same way to God as he himself has chosen. He does not even think of imposing anything on anyone, but what he strives for is for each person turning to him for help to take full responsibility for his relationship with God. The hermit on his part can support the other person through sacrifice and prayer. His attitude has therefore nothing to do with pretentiousness, but it is rather full of loving tenderness.

3. Living in Dialogue

Everybody belongs to himself and nobody can take possession of him without destroying the essential element of his personality, which is his freedom. The most distinctive feature of human nature consists in the natural desire to overcome oneself and to enter into a spiritual relationship with another person. Human freedom is founded on two indispensable pillars: the ability to possess oneself and the ability to overcome oneself. This is why every human being is, by his very nature, a person of dialogue and relationships. Both dialogue and relationships express the great potential for love of the human heart, a heart that is free.

The necessity of relationships

The seclusion and solitude that constitute the eremitic life do not aim at negating the fundamental dynamism of human existence, with its entering into dialogue and relationships. On the contrary, eremitic isolation and solitude form the basis of that dynamism. As was said, one of the most important motives for undertaking the life of the desert is the burning desire to find one's own identity. In the course of time, however, we discover that we are unable to realize that task unaided. The only way of learning anything important about oneself is to look at another person's face with love and attention.

As mentioned before, the hermit's solitude can never be a sign of withdrawal and isolation from the world and its affairs. The hermit, since he wants to serve other people, must arrive at a profound understanding of his own nature and his relation to God and the world. That is why his solitude is not at all a barrier, but it is rather an element that encourages openness towards others. The hermit, changed by the gift of meeting God, knows how to address the lonely hearts of those who come to seek his help and support. His solitude is not therefore a lifeless emptiness, but it is related to the most vital aspects of the human spirit. It is related to those spheres of human personality that can exist only if they are open to meet God and the world in love.

It so happens that in our times of political, cultural, and religious pluralism, the dialogue we enter and the openness, understanding, and acceptance we want to show determine the possibility of any constructive action. Christians will be trustworthy only inasmuch as they are people of dialogue and concord. John Paul II has set a great example of such a dialogue, inviting representatives of the world's main religions to Assisi in October, 1986. It was not theological matters, but the common thirst for peace, that gathered all those people to the hometown of St. Francis. The Dalai Lama, the Rabbi of Rome, Mother Teresa of Calcutta, and many others there were bound together in a community that became a prophetic sign, and a special encouragement for the whole world to pray for peace.

On that day the whole town of Assisi seemed to be one profound prayer, based on and inspired by a great range of venerated texts from the Sutras, the Bible, and the Koran. This testifying community of prayer, which united men and women of distant cultures, religious traditions, and confessions, all of them thirsting for peace in a world that is so very divided, was seen to proclaim something of fundamental importance. It showed that it could be possible to find a common root for all the religions, that will deepen the unity and the richness of all religious traditions. The Church, taking into consideration the common good, looks for ways of reaching universal consent and unity through Her efforts to build bridges of dialogue between the great religious traditions. In light of this, how pertinent are the words of outstanding Polish theologian Hryniewicz:

> Ecumenism broadens our horizons simply because it gives us access to the realms of spirituality and values that different religions cultivate. Nowadays, to be a Christian is to master a difficult art of evaluation that helps us accept others with all their diversities. That applies not only to our way of thinking, but also to the way in which we understand and live our whole life. ... To be a person of ecumenism and dialogue is like standing by the door of a house that is open to all differences and diversities. Without the capacity to accept differences we are limiting and impoverishing our own way of thinking and our existence.[50]

Of course, the event that took place in the town of St. Francis would never have happened if not for the spirit of openness and dialogue introduced by the last Vatican Council. In its document on the relation of the Church to non-Christian religions, the Council tries to show a common ground uniting all of the different spiritual traditions. After all, the fact that there are so many of them and their traditions are so diverse testifies to the common and often dramatic efforts undertaken to explain things ultimate and eternal. Each of the religious traditions poses questions about the human condition and identity, the aim of human life,

---

[50] W. Hryniewicz, *Pedagogia nadziei* (Warsaw, 1997), p. 129.

the source of good and evil, the purpose of suffering, and the prospect of human life after death in peace and happiness.

The Council believes that the Holy Spirit is at work also outside the visible confines of the Church. The seeds of truth have been disseminated abundantly on the different religious paths, which do not so much compete with one another as serve to make the ultimate fullness of Revelation given in Christ more distinct and intelligible. The Council states:

> The Catholic Church rejects nothing that is true and holy in these religions. She regards with sincere reverence those ways of conduct and of life, those precepts and teachings which, though differing in many aspects from the ones she holds and sets forth, nonetheless often reflect a ray of that Truth which enlightens all men. Indeed, she proclaims, and ever must proclaim Christ "the way, the truth, and the life" (Jn 14:6), in whom men may find the fullness of religious life, in whom God has reconciled all things to himself.[51]

A meeting that goes beyond differences

In the Declaration on Ecumenism the Vatican Council devoted much attention to the problem of dialogue. The document points to prayer and individual conversion (*metanoia*) as the indispensable conditions of any dialogue. A change of heart and holiness of life are the necessary conditions of authentic humility, love, and reverence towards those with whom we speak. It is prayer and conversion that are among the fundamental elements of eremitic life. That is

---

[51] The Second Vatican Council, *Declaration on the Relation of the Church to Non-Christian Religions (Nostra Aetate)*, par. 2.

why throughout history hermits have entered into dialogue not only with the people of the Church but also with the representatives of other religions.

The relationships between the Christian and Hindu traditions provide us with a good example of such dialogue. Jules Monchanin and Henri Le Saux, who lived at least for a certain time as hermits, were well known for their activities in this field. They promoted an attitude of openness and dialogue towards the religious tradition that is one of the oldest and most developed in human history. Their efforts have not remained unfruitful. Even if they did not establish many strong centers of the monastic life and did not cause many recognized conversions, they have certainly paved the way for mutual openness and dialogue.

Their chosen way of initiating dialogue was not based on the idea of specialists analyzing abstract problems. Instead, they themselves tried to gain a deeper insight into tradition by trying to carefully assimilate it in their own Christian lives. Their spiritual search was not easy, and there were many difficult moments when it appeared doubtful if any effective dialogue was possible at all. However, their relentless efforts prove that their great religious enthusiasm came from a deep desire to find fundamental values common to the two traditions. It is significant that they were fully aware of the difficulties that modern theological thought encounters. They knew the great role profound spiritual and mystical experience could play in bridging the gaps between the religious traditions. The example of these two Christian monks is a call for dialogue, concord, and mutual respect among men.

The life of Thomas Merton, a well-known Trappist hermit, is another example of how a Christian can come closer to a different tradition, namely Buddhism. Merton's journey to Bangkok in 1968, the journey that ended in his death, has been seen as a prophetic sign. He did not travel to the Far East as a missionary of his own spiritual tradition but, being aware of the deep crisis of contemporary Christian monasticism, Merton went as a pilgrim who wanted to learn something new that might be an asset for his own spirituality.

In his search, he met a lot of prominent figures of the Buddhist world, the most eminent of which were the Dalai Lama, D.T.Suzuki, and Thich Nhat Hanh. The famous Trappist made it clear that he was particularly interested in the Buddhist tradition of Zen, which he had chosen as the subject of several of his monographs. The dialogue between Merton and Suzuki, a prominent teacher of Zen who after World War II propagated that tradition in the Western world, is worth particular attention.

Their dialogue concerned, among other things, the Book of Genesis. One of the most important remarks they made is that a Buddhist seeking enlightenment (original nature) and a Christian striving for holiness (original justice) walk on paths with many analogies between them. Merton, with his characteristic flair, drew parallels between the stories of the masters of Zen and the sayings of the Christian Fathers of the desert; between Christian spiritual detachment and poverty and Buddhist emptiness; between the wisdom of the Cross and Buddhist *prajna* [insight]. Merton and Suzuki also discussed some other issues: purity of heart, innocence, and knowledge.[52]

Merton hoped for the possibility of reaching a mutual understanding and dialogue between people of different religious orientations by probing the deepest spiritual levels of human nature. Finding in the mature mystical life the most original human identity, we spontaneously sense the existential unity that we constitute together with all people and the world. The Trappist sees it thus:

> Behind, then, all that I have said is the idea that significant contacts are certainly possible and easy on the level of experience, not necessarily institutional monasticism, but among people who are seeking. The basic condition for this is that each be faithful to his own search. . . . And the deepest level of communication is not communication, but communion. It is wordless. It is beyond words, and it is beyond speech, and it is beyond concept. Not that we discover a new unity. We discover an older unity. My dear brothers, we are already one. But we imagine that we are not. And what we have to recover is our original unity.[53]

The Christian tradition, rich as it is, can enable us to make many efforts at dialogue and reconciliation. It is true to form that the fundamental condition of reaching authentic unity among people consists in their deep desire for truth and, consequently, for conversion of heart. All the

---

[52]   Cf. W. Johnston, op. cit., p.112.
[53]   T. Merton, *The Asian Journal of Thomas Merton* (London, 1974), pp. 307-308.

gaps and quarrels among people throughout history have in fact resulted from our sins, from our infidelity to God and to ourselves. The hermits, due to their particular way of life, play a special role in the recovery of unity among people. The upshot is that their solitude, silence, spirit of inner lowliness, and childlike faith placed in God and other people become the fertile soil for the many different initiatives that open people up to dialogue. Their simple and pure prayer, which comes straight from a sanctified heart, is a source of dialogue and mutual understanding.

4. The Concern for Ecology

The hermit is a person of dialogue and reconciliation, of understanding and friendship. His deep relationships with God and other people are reflected in his attitude towards the whole of creation. The Christian anchorite spends each of his days close to nature, enjoying its beauty and learning from it the fundamental lessons in life. He is a person who enthusiastically defends and cares for life because he knows its value and its ultimate meaning.

Killing the world

The spirit of exploitation and consumption that has dominated contemporary societies makes the hermit feel much pain. Modern people are faced with the danger of the destruction of nature and life. Great expanses of the natural world are being destroyed; forests, seas, and rivers are becoming desolate, more and more species are becoming extinct, and it seems that life is coming to an end. The exploitative approach that contemporary civilization takes towards nature, the well-planned conquest of the natural world, raises a specter of destruction and of the annihilation of life. Things that not so long ago were taken for success and a sign of progress now make us feel disappointed and ashamed. Having lost the true understanding of their own identity in relation to God and to others, people have also lost their respect towards God's creation.

When people become insensitive to the truth that is reflected in creation, they also lose the chance of coming closer to finding their own identity. After losing their original openness to the truth of the world, human hearts no longer have access to the refreshing fount of energy, the gift of God, that gushes from creation. That is why life is being destroyed: its structure and order have gone, its goodness and beauty are lost. The more people are taken in by the illusion that the exploitation of nature can be endless, the greater the risk and tragedy they bring upon themselves, making it also their own personal disaster. By destroying nature and running away from the natural world, people run away from themselves, as well as from their own freedom (which is a freely given gift) and their mission to develop and protect it. This new situation reaches the point of absurdity: the natural environment given to us as the environment of our growth and development is the cause of fear and frustration. The human spirit, now trapped, seems to have no way of escape. This was exactly Adam's situation the moment he realized the gravity of his sin.

Today, there are many who point to the Biblical text about human supremacy over the world (Gn 1:28) as a source of the contemporary ecological crisis. According to them, the

Bible propagates unlimited exploitation, brutal conquering, and harsh rulership over nature. But is this really true? Is it possible that the truth of the Bible not only serves to justify, but also directly motivates such destructive human attitudes? Is it not a tragic mistake and a great misunderstanding of the Scriptures?

St. Paul in his letter to the Romans (1:20-28) tells about the pitiful human hearts that are closed because of their sins. The situation described by the Apostle can undoubtedly be seen illustrated by people today, trapped in their selfish desires, for whom the mystery of the world remains completely inaccessible. Their sinful escape from the world and their attempts to seal themselves off in their own little world make them blind to the eternal order of values, blind to God and to the entire universe. The eremitic experience, deep as it can be, gives one an insight into the reality of the world and enables the hermit to unite himself with the world in the spirit of compassion and love. In this way, it becomes possible to accept the gift of creation and to appreciate the original source of everything, which is the mystery of Trinitarian Love.

The human being created in God's image was originally very sensitive to nature. The Biblical mission of supremacy over creation can only be understood correctly in light of the way in which God cares for it. God, seeing the goodness and beauty of His creation, of the whole world, incessantly supports its existence, cares for it, and guards it wisely. People in Paradise must have cultivated the Garden of Eden (Gn 2:15), cared for it and ruled over it in the proper sense of the word, because they lived in harmony with God. They lived in truth, matured in truth, and knew they were called to be in truth. But Adam's wise and just approach towards creation had nothing to do with the barbaric attitude that violates the elementary laws of nature in order to satisfy one's whims. As mentioned before, the world is as it were a cosmic sanctuary, so that people who consciously devastate it bear a grave responsibility before God and before history.

Sign of contradiction

It seems that there are many things that hermits, thanks to their specific experience, have to say to contemporary people faced with so many global ecological dangers. One cannot take the hermit to be an eccentric whose life is spent in a futile fight with evil. His spiritual wisdom enables him to look at the world not only in its practical aspects, but also as a gift of God Himself. That is why every element of the world contains an immeasurable value, which reflects God's creativity. Everything created enjoys its own unique place in the universe, and in the final moment of history it will be raised up to a new form of being in eternity. That is why every element of the creation has a deep meaning that surpasses the limits of space and time.

Eremitic life seems to be a sign of contradiction to a purely technical and pragmatic approach to the world that completely puts God and His logic aside. This approach needs to be healed, and the only way is through prayer and contemplation. The hermit who contemplates reality often becomes a wise teacher, able to provide others with a key to understanding the natural world. Eremitic life has always been a sign of contradiction in the face of thoughtless activity, and the frantic race for success, fame, and money. This way of life is a sign of contradiction to the brutal greed for power that poses a threat to creation.

The atmosphere of contemplation invites the hermit to reflect upon the affairs of the world and its current problems. Entering the path of meditation makes the heart sensitive and enables it to see clearly that every attempt at cutting off the natural ties between God and the world must inevitably end in tragedy. When somebody tries to cut creation off from God's original creative energy, it is not only an infringement on the inner structure of the natural world, but also an uprooting of humanity's natural support.

The simple and wise approach to the world that stems from the solitude and silence of eremitic life has nothing to do with the analytical approach of the scientist, but rather it is a compassionate and tender care filled with love, and with concern that springs from contemplation. After all, care for the world and its problems is concrete care for real persons. In fact, our sensitivity to the beauty of the world and our compassion for all its problems and anxieties are not something spontaneous. We need to make an effort to be sensitive and compassionate. Only then can we reach a sense of communion with the whole of creation; only then can we wisely and lovingly respect and support every form of life. Gratitude to God for the world and its original goodness and beauty is an important lesson that the hermit can teach contemporary people.

This different approach to the natural world depends on the extent to which we ourselves change our own approach to ourselves and to other people. Undoubtedly, all creatures are deeply related to one another. Their existences, greatly interwoven with one another, form a kind of communion and somehow determine human life. Creation is the fruit of God's limitless creativity, it is His "dance" and an echo of His eternity. This new sensitivity that we attain enables us to find God's footprints in the world, to see how the Lord reveals Himself in His creation and how creation is revealed in Him. What takes place here is a mutual relationship of love mediated by the Holy Spirit. The Spirit is God's breath that creates and sustains the world and that brings it to its final fulfillment. It is also the Spirit of love present in creation, the Spirit that continuously inspires hymns of praise and thanksgiving in human hearts.

The faith and hope present in the eremitic life are not born of isolation or hostility. On the contrary, they grow out of a love for creation, for the earth: the planet of people, animals, and plants, as S. Bulgakov describes beautifully:

> Oh, great mother, fertile soil! In thee we are born, on thee we feed, on thee we stamp our feet, to thee we return. Oh, children of the earth, love your mother, kiss her face tenderly, rinse her with your tears, sprinkle her with your sweat, moisten her with your blood and feed her with your bones! There is nothing that can be lost in her. She protects everything in her bosom; she, the silent memory of the world, provides everyone with fruit and life. If you do not love her, if you are not aware of her motherhood, you are a slave, a renegade, a pitiful rebel raising his hand against his mother, a devilish seed of nonexistence.[54]

---

[54] S. Bulgakov, *Свет невечерный. Созерцания и умозрения* (Moscow, 1917); quoted after W. Hryniewicz, *Zarys...*, op.cit., vol.3, p. 492. See also S. Bulgakow, op.cit., offset edition (Westmead, 1971), p. 188.

5. *Homo Socialis*

Today, among the different "signs of the times", we can notice that our contemporaries are very much conscious and concerned about their belonging to the great human family. Social concern for dealing with a whole range of problems such as famine, unemployment, war, torture, and prostitution seems to be their distinguishing feature. On the one hand, this kind of social consciousness results from the spirit of empathy and mercy towards the countless number of those in need. On the other hand, it is a form of "self-defense" against the greed and stupidity of those whose actions may eventually threaten all life on earth.

The logic of non-action

From such a perspective, the eremitic life may seem to be something totally anachronistic and contradictory to the Church's contemporary social involvement. Therefore, many are those who ask: how can you keep silent at a time when the world is being torn apart by wars and terror? How can you be so selfish as to enjoy spiritual rest and peace at a moment when our cities and neighborhoods suffer violence, terror, chaos, and frustration? Is it still possible for you today to devote yourself to contemplative prayer, which requires an atmosphere of inner concentration and solitude, and to remain as if indifferent to the pain of the millions who live in fear, subjected to the tyranny of power and money?

Contemporary hermits are often faced with charges like those above. The critics, however, do not necessarily have bad intentions. They often speak out because of their deep concern about the progress of good in the world. At first sight, all of the above arguments seem to be poignantly true. Yet on examining objectively the reality of the eremitic life as a whole – including motives for entering this kind of life, its day-to-day realization, its aspects of prayer and mystical experience – we can arrive at the conclusion that the charges are groundless.

As we have already mentioned, the eremitic life, as a part of the life of the Church, is a kind of charism, which means a gift given for the good of the whole Church community and also, in a broader sense, for the good of the whole world. The maturity of eremitic life should be measured neither by radical renunciation of the world, nor by strict observance of silence and fasting, though they are all indispensable elements in following properly the eremitic way of life. What testifies to the true maturity of one's eremitic vocation is his or her readiness to serve God, our brothers and sisters, and the whole world. But how exactly can a hermit show his commitment and concern for changing the world?

Most of the above questions have already been answered in this book. But perhaps we should now summarize the issues and look at them as a whole. What is really essential to point out is the prayerful and contemplative character of the eremitic life. Contemplative prayer experienced in solitude and silence is a form of adoring God and admiring His glory revealed in creation, and as such it leads us to deep inner change, which is conversion. As we change, we become more open and sensitive to any kind of suffering present in the world. The hermit is filled with compassion for every human misery and pain, so he remains united with all those who suffer and who are persecuted. What we have just said is not the author's fantasy or cheap sentimentality, but it is rather a realistic description of the heart awakened by the grace of the Holy Spirit. Through the light of the Spirit the hermit receives the gift of wisdom and understanding that allows him to get to the root of every problem, with little regard for changing trends and opinions.

Of course, the chief aim of prayer consists in adoration and praise of God's majesty. However, it also includes intercession and petition that are visibly effective in the world (Mt 7:7-12). The people of the Orient seem to have a much greater appreciation of the transforming power of meditation and prayer. That is why the monastic communities of the Orthodox Church, as well as those of India and Southern and Eastern Asia, are much more meditative and mystical in their character. The people of the East can still appreciate the power of simple meditative concentration, and they are still able to place a higher value on "non-action" that is genuinely committed than on activism with no spiritual roots. Of course, much is changing now, but many of these elements are still present in eastern cultures. Western civilization has lost much of its meditative and mystical elements, mainly because it has taken a pragmatic and technological orientation. That is probably why the eremitic life gives rise to so much controversy and anxiety.

The very presence of the hermit is a clear sign for those who have eyes to see and ears to hear. It is a sign that brings joy, encouragement, and hope to hearts that are lost and discouraged. The hermit's presence is above all a sign of God's love, the love that surpasses everything and is really active in the world. The action of this love is so effective and clear that there are people who try to understand it and to answer its call in a very simple, unambiguous way. The hermit, who has adopted the spiritual attitude of being like a child before God, is full of enormous vitality that stems from his inner integrity. Prayer shields him from the discouragement and resignation that are frequently experienced by those who are directly involved in the world's affairs. The spirit of prayer brings him joy and rest at the time of trials and temptations; it frees him from the jealousy and anger that lead to violence and destruction. The inner freedom and peace that the hermit emanates are a great gift for all those who come to him seeking his help or support.

However, if we were to narrow the eremitic life down to only passive contemplative prayer, we would miss some other characteristic traits of this vocation. The hermit does not only pray; he also reads, studies, and consults different people. He carefully observes the world in order to learn more about and to understand better its problems. Thus, the eremitic way has, so to speak, two tracks: one that is passive and the other that is active. They are complementary and depend on each other. If we had cut ourselves off from one of the two tracks, we would have inevitably deviated from the proper form of our vocation. Therefore, the silence, solitude, and spiritual nakedness have to be complemented by the positive dimension of life. That is why we need to perform acts of charity not towards an abstract idea of humanity, but rather towards particular people, towards those who suffer in the world today.

In the space of community

Undoubtedly, we have today a wide range of opportunities to undertake positive action in order to change the world. And certainly there is no doubt that the political and social problems of the contemporary world are so many and so complex that they go far beyond the ability and strength of any individual. We as humans feel, as it were, overburdened with the affairs of our everyday lives. What we are thus obliged to do is to make our choices in accordance with what the Holy Spirit tells us.

The efforts contemporary Christians make in order to establish justice, peace, and human solidarity frequently take the form of concrete political involvement and are often aimed at transforming social structures. Proclamation of the Good News cannot remain on the fringes of society, but it must rather approach directly all the problems that people face in their everyday experience. So the Church cannot become a kind of asylum, a safe place fenced in from brutal reality where we calm our fears, silence our worries, and in consequence begin to live an illusion. On the contrary, since the Church is a special place where the Spirit effectively gives Himself to us, She should animate the development of all the creative powers that lie dormant in us. She should stimulate us so that we can grow internally up to the point of final maturity, when we will love God and others in imitation of Christ, our Master and Friend.

What we have said about the Church applies also to the specific form of Church life that is the eremitic vocation. By offering his life to the service of God and man, the anchorite becomes a light that is to shine for all. As he leaves for the desert, the hermit paradoxically enters the heart of the world in order to show, by his poverty and simplicity, a new style and quality of existence that is achieved within the Church. It is an existence transformed by the gift of Christ's Passover, a life that radiates with wisdom, peace, and joy coming from the hermit's being close to his friends and to the beauty of nature. This is how the eremitic way becomes the leaven of creative faith and hope that makes it possible to effectively change a particular town, district, or village into a place of justice, friendship, and peace. Thus, the hermit's testimony also has its social significance.

By the nature of his vocation, the hermit stays away from any form of direct political action. As a matter of fact, he views it as ironic that some Christians have been caught up and dominated by politics. Fighting against communism, against the oppression of capitalism, or for environmental protection occupies them so much that they sometimes lose their common sense, not to mention the truth of the Gospel. The struggle against various forms of dictatorship and oppression in the world is motivated by the common awareness that every human being has his great and unique value. And it obviously requires people to organize themselves in different groups and communities. Planned, collective action is necessary, and this is just as indispensable here as it is for the people who work on improving economic and political structures so that societies can become more humane.

The inhabitant of a distant hermitage does not escape from the problems of everyday life. He wants to be the evangelical leaven that provides energy for changing people and societies. It was so in the past, and so it is at present. Hermits are people of passion and action. In order to transform reality, they concentrate rather on living in the spirit of the Beatitudes than on overthrowing political structures or lobbying for change. According to the hermit, it is possible to build a new world on the foundation of human hearts that are renewed by the Spirit and the truth, hearts that will show a new value and a new quality of human existence. He considers it possible to form a society based on the testimony given by small communities, communities that grow and develop through common celebration, work, love, contemplation, and the common joy of sharing.

The testimony given by people like Thomas Merton indicates that those who live in consecrated solitude and in the spirit of contemplation should also try to seek solutions to the world's social problems. One cannot authentically live in the spirit of Christian eremitism without searching continuously for new ways of realizing one's eremitic vocation for the good of other people and for the good of the world. These new ways and means have been indicated in the documents of the Second Vatican Council, so extraordinary in their content.

The hermit can do nothing if he tries unaided to change the world for the better. Promoting a sense of human solidarity, he wants to enter into a direct dialogue with others in order to arrive at unity and peace in the whole human family. No hermit is allowed, by the very fact of choosing his way of life, to escape from the world. What he should strive for is not to escape from the world, but rather to minister to it, on behalf of its development, progress, and finally its salvation. He understands his vocation as the service of love, rendered with unique empathy and compassion for the whole of creation.

Thus the eremitic testimony, meaningful as it is, does not refer to any special form of social or political action. The hermit usually shows no interest in this kind of activity. His testimony is clear and effective because of the consistency of his life decisions made in the service of God and mankind.

The hermit is a person of prayer who reaches his identity not through action, but rather through entrusting himself consciously and unconditionally to Christ. That is probably why the eremitic identity is so inaccessible and unacceptable for those who value other people only for their achievements. What the eremitic life is all about is not the quantity of achievements but the quality of existence, which is to remain a mystery. St. John the Baptist, the great leader of all who dwell in the desert, can serve as a model representing such an attitude in the eremitic life:

> And yet the bridegroom's friend, who stands there
> and listens, is glad when he hears the bridegroom's
> voice. This same joy I feel, and now it is complete.
> He must increase, but I must decrease. (Jn 3:29-30)

That is why the hermit does not actually have to do anything special; his mission, paradoxically, is that of "non-action". He offers a sacrifice of his life by persevering in silent concentration and attentive love before the Lord. We should stress here that the willing and joyful readiness to offer oneself to God, the readiness to accept every form of suffering out of love for God and people, is eventually so powerful that nothing can stop it from changing the world .

Christians living in solitude, as well as those who because of God's calling remain in the great wilderness of contemporary cities, have the same ultimate aim. In entering the way of their Master, they do not want to be served, but to serve others, and to give their lives for the salvation of the world. Only such an attitude can prove the Christian mission to be trustworthy and truthful, because its meaning is not determined by any immediate success. The meaning of the

Christian mission can be seen only in the perspective of eternity.

6. Not by Bread Alone

There are certainly more things that contemporary people are hungry for than bread, grain, wine, and fruit. In prosperous countries, despite their ample social welfare, people are still full of fear and frustration; they seem to long for something that will satisfy their inner needs and desires. It must then be something immeasurable, but at the same time very real, that is as essential to human life as the air we breathe and the bread we eat.

Everybody knows that nowadays people feel terribly lonely. On the one hand, in political and economic terms the world keeps uniting. On the other hand, however, people feel more and more isolated from one another. Contemporary people feel that they are lost, unattended, and unimportant amidst the bustle of everyday matters. They pass by one another, all of them so similar, in complete anonymity, and only from time to time do they stop to say the meaningless "How are you?" The societies of today seem to be made up of millions of independent atoms that are, so to speak, impregnable to one another. They run into one another once in a while, but only to bounce back and to go on their individual independent tracks again.

The light of trust and the gift of peace

Love, faith, hope, and friendship are the great treasures that everybody longs for. What the hermit wants to give others is not money or bread. The gift he has to offer is the trust and faith he puts in others, in everybody who knocks at his door. This gift is very personal, and it is not addressed to some anonymous crowd but directly to the heart that longs for mutual presence, dialogue, and meeting. The hermit offers his charity and faith in complete openness and trust, in the same way in which he himself has been accepted and embraced by the Father's arms. The hermit embraces everyone with his acceptance and trust not because they deserve it but simply because they are in need of it. The hermit's hope and trust imitate God's, who has not hesitated to grant us freedom.

Trust is thus the fruit of love. Its warm and delicate light is able to open human hearts, even those that have been badly wounded. Through the trust the hermit puts in others, he can open before them the way of faith, hope, and charity, the way on which they can meet God. God alone is the One who can satisfy man's dire and unmet need of love, faith, and peace, because He is the natural source of all values. People who trust each other are those who love, talk to, and are close to each other, those who give each other peace, kindness, and a smile. Trust overcomes all division and crushes our egoism and sin. In the community of those who trust one another, cruelty, hatred, and war live no longer and peace is born.

An authentic meeting with Christ gives birth to peace in the human heart. By touching the mystery of the Passover, the hermit is introduced into the realm of the spiritual fruit of Christ's death and resurrection, where peace seems to be one of the most precious of gifts. For the hermit, peace is the fruit of his long-lasting hardship and toil, of the falls and victories that for many years have marked his everyday life. The practice of prayer, the rigors of solitude, silence, and fasting, help the human spirit to become open to the divinizing light of Tabor, the light that, if accepted, brings spiritual joy and peace.

The peace of the desert, therefore, has nothing to do with the shallow psychological composure achieved through relaxation. It is rather an expression of the real power of Christ, the power that comes from the experience of Passover. Peace is one of the finest fruits of the Spirit, Who takes up His dwelling in the humble and quiet heart. This is the peace that brings Christians to reconciliation with God, with the world, and finally with themselves.

The peace of Christ cannot be achieved at the moment when two hostile powers reach military balance, nor can it be obtained by the crazy means of an arms race, nor by terrorizing the enemy. The peace of Christ results from a struggle insofar as that means the spiritual struggle against our pride, stupidity, and hypocrisy, the struggle for freedom. Freedom is so valuable because it is born when we truly and unconditionally invite God into every single moment of our everyday lives. By doing so, we are able to accept in love all our weakness, fragility, and insufficiency.

Christians want to make peace in order to spread the radical "revolution" brought by the transforming light of the Gospel. Any attempts to overcome the darkness of sin, ignorance, indifference, and hypocrisy are not in vain. Having renounced all violence, the hermit delicately and mercifully sows the seeds of the lasting peace that comes from Christ's Paschal victory. The way of peace paved with solitude and silence is not the "way of the sword" but "the way of the Cross", leading through the shame and the glory of the Cross.

Conclusion

The logic of Christian faith is rooted and centered in the love that the Father has granted us in His Son. The fullness of truth revealed in Christ is the gift of His love for us. Love's wisdom and its original beauty are still present and visible throughout human history. Christ accepts the human condition in order to fill it with a new light and power that stem from the victory of Easter morning. Everyday human life, enlightened thus with the brightness of the Resurrection, is now put in a new perspective, and it gains new values, goals, and meanings. It is so because in meeting us in faith, God reaches to the most original elements of our existence. Christ always looks at the most intimate spheres of our lives, and He leaves there a lasting mark that will speak "for" or "against" us.

All cultures know people who step back from the usual course of everyday life and choose solitude in order to find the full meaning of their own existence. Thus, the way of Christian solitude is not darkened with the shadow of loneliness, for essentially it always leads to a personal presence, a dialogue and a meeting with God and with other people. Basically, the eremitic vocation can be summarized as following obediently the voice of the Father, who leads us out into the desert so that Jesus can become the only object of our thoughts, desires, and love. The eremitic experience of solitude comes down to the Paschal Mystery of Christ, the Mystery in which shame, poverty, and nakedness paradoxically bring about the fullness of life. The hermit consciously lives on the outskirts of society. The more he deliberately becomes useless and the more he stresses the logic of God's Kingdom, the more he reveals the futility of life narrowed down to a "time of misery". Thomas Merton wrote:

> Also it seems to me that the solitary life fulfils the above texts by the abandonment of the Psalmist: "But I am a beggar and poor: the Lord is careful for me." (39:18) We live in constant dependence upon this merciful kindness of the Father, and thus our whole life is a life of gratitude – a constant response to his help which comes to us at every moment. I think everyone finds this out in any vocation, provided it is his true vocation.[55]

Undoubtedly, the eremitic life can be characterized by the struggle undertaken in order to learn the truth of our existence in the light of Christ's grace. In such a perspective, the eremitic vocation takes on a form of prophecy, which means that the clear testimony it gives becomes a signpost for all those who want to find the seeds of truth sown throughout the world.

This book originated as an attempt to describe a few basic concepts that relate directly to the rich and mysterious reality of the eremitic life. As the perspective that we have sketched here remains an unfathomable mystery and a drama of two freedoms – the human and the divine – the intuitions we have presented do not pretend to give a thorough description

---

[55] T. Merton, *Thoughts in Solitude* (New York, 1958), p. 107.

of the phenomenon. They are also not intended to clarify satisfactorily all doubts about the human experience. What they rather aim at is to strike some spiritual sparks that will brighten up some of the darkness of the Mystery. The rest is silence.